D1015765

CONTEMPORARY ISSUES

Issues in
Sports

by Stephen Currie

Lucent Books, San Diego, CA

Other books in the Contemporary Issues series:

Biomedical Ethics
The Environment

Library of Congress Cataloging-in-Publication Data

Currie, Stephen, 1960–
    Issues in sports / by Stephen Currie.
        p. cm.—(Contemporary issues)
    Includes bibliographic references (p.   ) and index.
        ISBN 1-56006-477-3 (alk. paper)
    1. Sports—United States—Sociological aspects. I. Title.
    II. Series: Contemporary issues (San Diego, Calif.)
GV706.5.C86 1998
306.4'83'0973—dc21   97-27451
                                                                CIP
                                                                AC

TABLE OF CONTENTS

Foreword

When men are brought face to face with their opponents, forced to listen and learn and mend their ideas, they cease to be children and savages and begin to live like civilized men. Then only is freedom a reality, when men may voice their opinions because they must examine their opinions.

—Walter Lippmann, American editor and writer

CONTROVERSY FOSTERS DEBATE. The very mention of a controversial issue prompts listeners to choose sides and offer opinion. But seeing beyond one's opinions is often difficult. As Walter Lippmann implies, true reasoning comes from the ability to appreciate and understand a multiplicity of viewpoints. This ability to assess the range of opinions is not innate; it is learned by the careful study of an issue. Those who wish to reason well, as Lippmann attests, must be willing to examine their own opinions even as they weigh the positive and negative qualities of the opinions of others.

The *Contemporary Issues* series explores controversial topics through the lens of opinion. The series addresses some of today's most debated issues and, drawing on the diversity of opinions, presents a narrative that reflects the controversy surrounding those issues. All of the quoted testimonies are taken from primary sources and represent both prominent and lesser-known persons who have argued these topics. For example, the title on biomedical ethics contains the views of physicians commenting on both sides of the physician-assisted suicide issue: Some wage a moral argument that assisted suicide allows patients to die with dignity, while others assert that assisted suicide violates the Hippocratic oath. Yet the book also includes the opinions of those who see the issue in a more personal way. The relative of a person who died by assisted suicide feels the loss of a loved one and makes a plaintive cry against it, while companions of another assisted suicide victim attest that their friend no longer wanted to endure the agony of a slow death. The profusion of quotes illustrates the range of thoughts and emotions that impinge on any debate. Displaying the range of perspectives, the series is designed to show how personal belief—whether informed by statistical evidence, religious conviction, or public opinion—shapes and complicates arguments.

Each title in the *Contemporary Issues* series discusses multiple controversies within a single field of debate. The title on environmental issues, for example, contains one chapter that asks whether the Endangered Species Act should be repealed, while another asks if Americans can afford the economic and social costs of environmentalism. Narrowing the focus of debate to a specific question, each chapter sharpens the competing perspectives and investigates the philosophies and personal convictions that inform these viewpoints.

Students researching contemporary issues will find this format particularly useful in uncovering the central controversies of topics by placing them in a moral, economic, or political context that allows the students to easily see the points of disagreement. Because of this structure, the series provides an excellent launching point for further research. By clearly defining major points of contention, the series also aids readers in critically examining the structure and source of debates. While providing a resource on which to model persuasive essays, the quoted opinions also permit students to investigate the credibility and usefulness of the evidence presented.

For students contending with current issues, the ability to assess the credibility, usefulness, and persuasiveness of the testimony as well as the factual evidence given by the quoted experts is critical not only in judging the merits of these arguments but in analyzing the students' own beliefs. By plumbing the logic of another person's opinions, readers will be better able to assess their own thinking. And this, in turn, can promote the type of introspection that leads to a conviction based on reason. Though *Contemporary Issues* offers the opportunity to shape one's own opinions in light of competing or concordant philosophies, above all, it shows readers that well-reasoned, well-intentioned arguments can be countered by opposing opinions of equal worth.

Critically examining one's own opinions as well as the opinions of others is what Walter Lippmann believes makes an individual "civilized." Developing the skill early can only aid a reader's understanding of both moral conviction and political action. For students, a facility for reasoning is indispensable. Comprehending the foundations of opinions leads the student to the heart of controversy—to a recognition of what is at stake when holding a certain viewpoint. But the goal is not detached analysis; the issues are often far too immediate for that. The *Contemporary Issues* series induces the reader not only to see the shape of a current controversy, but to engage it, to respond to it, and ultimately to find one's place within it.

Introduction

The Real Versus the Ideal

SPORTS COMPETITION IS AS OLD as humanity itself. The ancient Greeks launched the original Olympic Games. The Romans built the Colosseum, an enormous sports palace that served as the world's first multipurpose stadium. In Central America, the Aztecs and the Maya played ball games of various types. The sport of lacrosse has its roots among the Eastern Woodland peoples of North America, and martial arts competitions have been going on for many generations in eastern Asia. From Kenya to Australia, from Hawaii to Spain, sports have been a part of the lives of people everywhere.

At its best, sport is a pure contest of athletic skill and power. Ideally, participants do not take unfair advantage of their opponents (thus the word "sportsmanship"). Athletes work hard, show respect, and give their all in every competition. Sports are designed to show off the best of human achievement. The winner is honored, but the loser is not dishonored. Spectators admire the grace, talent, and determination of every athlete. In the ideal world, this is the way things would be.

Unfortunately, the world is not an ideal place, and neither is the domain of sport. In reality, the ideal of competition has been corrupted in many different ways. Indeed, most of the current controversies about sports are questions about how well the ideal of sport matches the reality. All too often, the two do not mesh. If athletes are to show sportsmanship and restraint on the field, then it becomes difficult to justify trash-talking in the National Basketball Association and dances after goals in World Cup soccer. If the loser is to be applauded for skills and effort, then it is hard to understand why even second-place finishers are considered failures in many sports today.

Violence offers another good example of the split between the ideal and the real. During a National Hockey League game between the Detroit Red Wings and the Colorado Avalanche in 1997, players viciously slammed each other into the boards, used their sticks as weapons, and squared off in several fights. A journalist described the game as a "bloodbath." The referees, however, did not call an unusually large number of penalties, and the league did little to punish the players involved in the violence. People expect ice hockey to be bruising. Still, there is a difference between playing hard and attempting to hurt an opponent. Many players in that 1997 game showed disrespect for opponents, safety, and rules. The NHL's weak response struck some observers as an endorsement of mindless violence—and a corruption of the ideal of sports.

Another controversy involves race. In April 1997, fifty years after Jackie Robinson broke the color barrier in professional baseball, mixed-race golfer Tiger Woods became the first nonwhite to win the Masters golf championship. Woods's victory, while applauded by many fans, drew attention to the situation of African Americans in sports today. Top-ranked minority golfers and tennis players, for example, traditionally have been few and far between.

Tiger Woods is the first non-white to win the Masters Gold Championship. His success called attention to the racism that blacks have experienced in the sport.

Even in sports where many or most athletes are black, inequity in the front office persists. Few head coaches or general managers of sports teams are African American, for instance.

And a third example is the role of money in sports today. For many years, stock car racing was a minor sport, with a small but devoted group of fans who cheered on their favorite drivers at tracks in out-of-the-way towns like North Wilkesboro, North Carolina. Then corporations discovered that they could make money by sponsoring drivers and advertising on race broadcasts. Fans outside the Southeast began to follow the sport. Stock car racing hit the big time. Suddenly, the North Wilkesboro Speedway was considered too small, too rickety, and too isolated to help sell the sport to new fans and advertisers. Despite racing's long history in North Wilkesboro, the stock car circuit pulled out. Instead of valuing loyalty and tradition, the leaders of the sport chose to value money. A journalist identified one effect of the national stock car racing association's action as follows: "In NASCAR's rush uptown, the essence of the sport is disappearing at breakneck speed."

Of course, controversy and extremes are nothing new for sports. In Victorian England, spectacles such as six-day bicycle races and bare-knuckle prizefighting were common. Fans crowded into steamy arenas and cramped stadiums to see if competitors would collapse from exhaustion or injury. Many did. While some interpreted these events as celebrations of human endurance, others called them ghoulish and uncivilized. In America, the early days of baseball were filled with players who cheated while the umpire's back was turned: going from first base to third base without bothering to touch second, for instance, or blocking a runner who was trying to score. Some fans felt that the constant cheating made baseball less than a true sport. And when the modern Olympic Games began nearly a century ago, social class won out over athleticism as an ideal: the only athletes allowed to compete were those wealthy enough not to have to work for a living. At various times sport has been polluted by greed, by vengeance, by a win-at-all-costs mentality—and much more.

The ideal, in fact, may never have existed. Perhaps all sports, at all times, have been tainted with politics, bigotry, or brutality. And

A NASCAR stock car race under way at Daytona International Speedway. Many fans believe the sport has lost its small town appeal because of corporate sponsorship.

perhaps the ideal never can be reached. Still, it makes sense to try to keep our sports as pure as possible. The controversies described in this book are about how closely the reality of sport matches the ideal. They are debates about what sport is, what sport can be, and—most of all—about what sport should be.

Chapter 1

Do Organized Sports Demand Too Much of Children?

W HEN RYAN JARONCYK WAS five years old, his father, Bill, signed him up to play baseball in a local youth league. It was clear to everyone who saw him in action that even at that young age, Ryan was an exceptional athlete: fast, strong, and graceful, with excellent eye-hand coordination. Over the next thirteen years, Jaroncyk's skills continued to improve. He dominated each league he played in, much to the delight of his father, a former college football player. By high school, Jaroncyk was spending most of his time playing shortstop, a key defensive position and one he played very well.

As he grew older, Jaroncyk's play brought him media attention and plenty of interest from professional scouts. In 1995 a sports magazine called him the second best high school shortstop in the nation. Shortly after his graduation from high school, the New York Mets chose him with their first pick in major league baseball's annual draft. He was the eighteenth player selected overall. Jaroncyk immediately signed a contract with the Mets that called for a bonus payment of $850,000 and a $100,000 scholarship fund. Most observers predicted a bright future for him.

But in the spring of 1997, while working his way up through baseball's minor leagues, Jaroncyk abruptly announced that he was quitting the sport for good. In a four-page letter to the Mets' general manager, he explained that he had never liked baseball. The game simply moved along too slowly for him; there was never enough

11

action. "I always thought it was boring," he said. Jaroncyk, it turned out, had tried to quit baseball several times, including once as a high school junior, but his father had always talked him out of it. Indeed, according to Jaroncyk, he had stuck with baseball only because of his parents. "I don't want to blame anybody," he said about his sports career as a child, "but I didn't feel I had many choices."

The Mets accepted Jaroncyk's retirement with grace. The team has not asked him to return his signing bonus or his college fund. Mets officials say they knew of problems between Ryan and his father at the time of the draft. They were aware that Bill Jaroncyk had yelled at Ryan during Ryan's games, and both parents acknowledged to a Mets scout that the father often put pressure on the son to excel. Still, the Mets hadn't realized how deep the issues ran. "We just thought he had an overbearing dad," the scout said later, "and Ryan just needed to get away from the house."

Organized sports for kids are supposed to be fun. For Ryan Jaroncyk, however, organized baseball was anything but fun. Jaroncyk did not play ball for his own enjoyment. Instead, he played for his father. "I felt a lot of pressure to keep playing," he said afterward. As a high school student, he grew interested in football. But when he was hurt during a game, his parents reminded him that injuries could ruin his chances for a professional baseball career.

Ten Most Popular Boys' High School Sports	
	Participants
1. Football	957,507
2. Basketball	544,025
3. Track & Field (Outdoor)	444,248
4. Baseball	457,937
5. Soccer	296,587
6. Wrestling	227,596
7. Cross-Country	174,599
8. Golf	150,578
9. Tennis	132,451
10. Swimming and Diving	93,523

Ten Most Popular Girls' High School Sports	
	Participants
1. Basketball	447,687
2. Track & Field (Outdoor)	385,605
3. Volleyball	370,957
4. Softball (Slow Pitch)	313,607
5. Soccer	226,636
6. Tennis	150,346
7. Cross-Country	145,624
8. Swimming & Diving	123,886
9. Field Hockey	56,502
10. Track & Field (Indoor)	49,365

Source: National Federation of High School Associations, 1996–97.

Jaroncyk immediately gave up football. Looking back on his childhood, Jaroncyk blames part of his distaste for baseball on the way his father pushed him to succeed. "I love my dad very much," he said after his retirement. "He really wanted the best for me, but he went about it the wrong way." From the age of five, Jaroncyk was on the fast track to the majors—whether he wanted to be or not.

According to some observers, Jaroncyk's story, while extreme, is not uncommon. "One too often sees young athletes with worried, bored and robotic looks," writes a sports psychologist who believes that adults have taken most of the fun out of organized youth sports. From baseball to soccer, from tennis to gymnastics, many adults express concern about the way children's athletics programs are set up and practiced. By definition, youth sports ought to have the interests of children at heart. At their best, they do. Ryan Jaroncyk, however, can testify to some of the negative effects of organized sports on young athletes. Upon retiring, he and his wife packed all his baseball equipment into a box and dropped it in the garbage. "I feel very happy," he said afterward.

Professional Sports for Children

Nearly everyone agrees that youth sports can be valuable for children. Thousands of children enjoy participating in organized leagues. When two thousand youth hockey players were asked what they disliked most about their sport, nearly half said they had nothing at all to complain about. Sports provide discipline, both mental and physical. Participating in sports keeps kids active, which is good for their health, and ideally teaches them about teamwork, determination, and sportsmanship, which helps them in life. And most important of all, sports are supposed to be fun.

If youth sports were always fun and pressure-free, there would be little or no debate about them. However, as Ryan Jaroncyk's story demonstrates, youth sports are about much more than fresh air and cooperation. They are also about professional contracts, parental egos, and local or even national fame. Too often, youth sports seem to be less for children than for adults. In some cases, children's roles are to live out the dreams of parents, coaches, and even entire communities. The result is children who play to please adults, who feel

Many critics claim sports like Pop Warner football are tainted by a spirit of winning at any cost.

they must win at all costs, and for whom sports is no longer any fun. "We've created an atmosphere of professional sports for children," says a youth sports administrator.

There is evidence to back this argument. In a few sports, notably women's figure skating, tennis, and gymnastics, young teenagers

are professionals. In women's gymnastics, virtually no serious competitor lasts beyond the age of twenty. Many find their careers are over well before they turn eighteen. In a few other sports, such as basketball and football, athletes of high school age and even lower are often lionized by their communities; they are not technically professionals, but the pressures put

China's Gway-Suk Kim performs in the 1992 Olympics. Gymnastics has been criticized for allowing girls to compete at a very young age.

on them are similar to what professionals face. Coaches and parents from swimming to soccer send children messages, intentional or not, about the importance of winning. Many athletes who starred as children look back on their successes and realize that something was missing. "It wasn't fun, I'll tell you that," said a man who had had a successful baseball career as a child.

"Toxic Adults"

The basic problem of youth sports, according to some experts, lies in what one writer has called "toxic adults." At worst, a toxic adult is a coach or parent who, like Bill Jaroncyk, sees a young athlete as an extension of himself. Every sport seems to have a few: coaches who bully players, parents who push children to do more than the kids can handle, fans who curse umpires over calls they don't like. These adults can make it difficult for the child to enjoy the games; sometimes, they can make it next to impossible for a child to quit playing.

Perhaps the biggest issue is pushy parents. Teenage figure skater Tara McGarvey speaks of a fellow skater whose parents are focused on their daughter's career to the exclusion of almost everything else.

According to McGarvey, the girl doesn't attend school, has no friends off the skating rink, and has never had a birthday party. "She hasn't had a life, basically," McGarvey says. Golfer Beverly Klass was nine years old when she turned professional in 1965 but never made it big in the sport, in part because of her father, who beat her when she didn't want to practice and screamed at her during competitions. "It made me feel pretty bad," she said years later. "I got so I didn't want to play."

Overzealous parents have been a problem for other athletes too. The father of tennis star Mary Pierce was banned from attending events on the women's pro tour because of persistent verbal abuse of the young player. And appalling behavior is all too common even among parents of the youngest children. One writer mentions a father who hit his six-year-old with a wrench after the boy lost a motorcycle race. Tara McGarvey once saw a woman slap her four-year-old daughter's face—because the girl finished second in a skating competition.

Coaches can take away from children's enjoyment as well. "Coaches who are entirely negative have kids who don't play next year," says one expert. Many observers see plenty of coaches like this, who substitute insults for instruction and emphasize winning over fun. "They treat twelve-year-old boys like animals," says a woman about youth football league coaches in her state. A youth soccer coach writes about fellow coaches who schedule more practices than league rules allow—at their own homes, so authorities will not find out. Children who complain are kicked off the team.

Older Children

The problem of toxic adults extends to athletes of high school age. Many top teenage athletes are under enormous pressure to win, and adults around them seem to stop at nothing to make it happen. To prepare their young charges for the Olympics, girls' gymnastics coaches usually require thirty to fifty hours of practice a week. Many of the young gymnasts drop out of school (and take correspondence courses) because they are unable to manage a regular course load and train at the same time. Such long hours of work also can cause serious injuries, but gymnasts' careers are short, and instead of insisting on lengthy recuperation periods, coaches routinely require students to continue to train despite their pain—and

A Little League pitcher gets direction from his coach. Do such organized sports teams teach young children that winning is everything?

the potential for even more serious physical damage. Eating disorders are common among elite gymnasts, too. Competitors must be unusually light to succeed, and many coaches order their sudents to take off pounds no matter what the consequences.

Team sports suffer from some of the same issues. In Rhode Island, a high school soccer team was stripped of a state title when it was discovered that the team was using a player who had graduated the year before. He had been playing under another student's name, with the support and knowledge of the team's coaches. In New York City, outstanding basketball players who can barely read are recruited by high schools across the metropolitan area. In too many sports programs, young athletes are taught that winning is everything, and from this they also conclude that health, education, honesty, and fair play are unimportant, and that games are not meant to be fun—an obvious corruption of the ideal of sports.

Stress is another issue. In many places successful teenage athletes are admired, even idolized. This adulation strikes some as misplaced. It can be hard for teenagers to live up to the dreams of an entire community. A writer notes that there are several histories of the city of Odessa, Texas, but none are as long and detailed as a

High school students celebrate the victory of their team. High school athletes are often well known and admired in their community. Critics claim that this places too much stress on young people.

book about one of Odessa's high school football teams. In some Indiana towns, stores and restaurants close up when the high school basketball team is playing, because nearly everyone goes to the game. And in gymnastics and figure skating, a young competitor must often carry the weight of representing an entire country.

Opposing Views

A few observers see the pressure of youth sports as a positive influence on kids. "That's what life is all about anyway, pressure and competition," says one of the players on the team that won the Little League championship in 1954. "I'd like my son to go through what I went through," he adds. "It would be good for him." Some successful athletes agree. They thrived on the pressure, or at least learned to handle it, and are now proud of their achievements. "You don't hear too many complaints from the winners," comments gymnast Mary Lou Retton, who won an Olympic gold medal as a teenager.

Other experts say that excessive pressure is not a serious problem and that the presence of "toxic adults" is overblown. "Countless children have enjoyed adult-sponsored sports," writes one observer. Several studies support this perspective. One examined the comments made by Little League coaches to their players and found that about 97 percent were positive. Another tracked what spectators at games were saying in the stands, and heard few negative comments. While it is fashionable to look back on the "good old days" when, as one writer put it, "ten-year-olds played dodge ball and red rover, not select team soccer," some people involved in youth sports point out that kid-organized games were far from paradise. "How many children have been left out of pickup games?" one writer asks. "How many children have been bullied by older children? Beaten? Terrified?"

As for the emphasis placed by communities on youth sports, many observers argue that it is not all bad. "I've been on the City Council," says a man who once played basketball for Durfee High in Fall River, Massachusetts. "I've run for mayor. I've had successful businesses. But people around here still look at me as a Durfee basketball player."

A young girl listens to directions during a Pop Warner game. Supporters believe such organized sports are positive community programs that teach children discipline and commitment.

Looking back, he calls his time on the team "probably the best days of my life." High school and Little League sports, some argue, bring communities together in a positive way, giving youngsters a chance to shine and feel they belong. "I'd do it all over again," says a high school football player who never made the pros.

Moreover, according to some coaches and parents, exceptional young athletes are aware of the dangers and drawbacks of youth sports. In this view, children who cut back on their social lives for their sports, risk injury for a chance at a gold medal, or move halfway across the country to get first-class coaching are making informed choices that adults are bound to respect. "I want children pushed to their potential," says one father. Whether their potential lies in football, piano, or computer programming, he adds, "it's not fair not to do that for them."

Coaches, especially, often see young athletes as exceptional people whose talent and inner drive to achieve set them apart from more ordinary children. "Shannon has done exactly what she's wanted to do," says Steve Nunno, who coached two-time Olympic gymnast Shannon Miller.

Coach Steve Nunno comforts an unhappy Shannon Miller during the 1996 Olympics.

"She gave up nothing. She did it her way." It is common for high school coaches to describe focused athletes as "16 going on 30." Some young athletes agree. A few observers have charged that pressure from adults forced gymnast Dominique Moceanu, who was fourteen years old during the 1996 Atlanta Olympics, to give up her childhood for her sport. Moceanu, however, says that competing was her own decision. "I have the rest of my life to have a childhood," she adds.

When Kids' Sports Work

The strongest evidence for the value of youth sports is the example set by athletes such as golfer Tiger Woods, baseball player Alex Rodriguez, and swimmer Janet Evans, who have had remarkable success at young ages without losing their focus or becoming arrogant. The lives of athletes such as these give experts hope for the future. While there are many gymnasts, football players, and skaters who burn out early, suffer abuse, or get swelled heads, there are others who keep a sense of balance in their lives. That sense of balance, psychologists and many parents say, is critical if a child is to grow up happy and healthy—and indeed, to be the best athlete they can be. "If they're not a whole person," says Debra McGarvey, mother of figure skater Tara, "they can't be a whole athlete."

Achieving a sense of balance, while difficult, is far from impossible. The most important step, says sports psychologist Sean McCann, is to make certain the young athlete lives in a home that is "family centered" rather than "child centered." In a family-centered home, the athlete is no more important than any other family member; in a child-centered family, the star and his needs come first. Even if a child is unusually talented, agrees psychologist Matt Mitchell, "that doesn't mean the youngster should be exempted from contributing to the family and doing the 'normal' things he would have been doing if he weren't athletically inclined."

Parents are responsible for setting the proper tone. Don't carry a star tennis player's equipment, advises one tennis coach; don't let your child rely on you to wake her for early morning practices, suggests the father of a talented swimmer. Foremost among these guidelines is making sure the child has fun. "If you don't build a good base of fun and enjoyment," cautions psychologist McCann, "you're at a much higher risk for producing a kid who has burnout issues."

Indeed, some of the best-adjusted athletes have had parents who limited their practice time and made them do other things as well. Tennis star Martina Hingis was the best player in the world by age sixteen. Still, she is said to average under two hours a day of tennis practice and is noted for a good attitude as well as plenty of success. Columnist Joan Ryan writes of a gymnast who never made the Olympics but limited her training, did not starve herself while she was a competitor, and reached adulthood with a good education, a healthy body, and an undamaged psyche. And San Francisco 49ers quarterback Steve Young says he never seriously considered a professional football career until late in college; "I just focused on having fun," he explains.

Experts also say that parents need to respect children's choices—an area where Ryan Jaroncyk's parents had particular difficulty. The option to quit should always be available. Martina

Martina Hingis celebrates her victory in the U.S. Open. Martina's mother claims that she does not push Martina to maintain the rigorous schedule such success demands, but lets her make the choice.

Hingis's mother insists that Martina always had the choice of tennis or school and could have given up tennis with no consequences. "If I want to quit skating," says Tara McGarvey, "all I have to do is say, 'Mom, I want to quit.'" Not all elite child athletes have this much choice in the matter. If they did, there might be less controversy about the role of children in sports.

Suggestions

Some recent changes and proposed changes might reduce some of the excesses of youth sports. Gymnastics, tennis, and figure skating have established minimum age limits, typically fifteen or sixteen, for certain high-profile tournaments and competitions. Such regulations will not, of course, help to limit practice sessions for very young athletes, but they will keep children from the pressures of heavy competition a bit longer. There are increasing numbers of training programs designed to teach coaches and officials of youth sports teams about children's emotional and physical development. Some programs also include parents of young athletes. A few observers have suggested that the training sessions be made mandatory for all coaches, volunteer or paid, down to the lowest level of organized sports. Whether this will happen, though, remains to be seen.

In an ideal world, youth sports would not be overemphasized. Ideally, the kids who play sports would do it for fun and for the joy of competition, not for medals, not for fear of the consequences of letting somebody down. Ideally, parents would take their cues from their children where athletics is concerned. High schools would hold pep rallies for math students, young writers, and the school orchestra as well as for the football team. Coaches would ease up on workouts. Ideally, society would recognize that child athletes are children first and athletes only second.

As Ryan Jaroncyk's story demonstrates, all it takes is one pushy, misguided parent or overzealous, dictatorial coach to ruin a child's fun—and perhaps physical and emotional health as well. "We expect sacrifices to be made in the name of great success," writes Joan Ryan. "But when the sacrifices mean a childhood spent in the toils of physical and psychological abuse, the price is too high." Thankfully, few young athletes are damaged so severely by youth sports. But for the sake of the children, observers are increasingly suggesting that if errors in guidance are made, it is preferable to find that capable athletes have been held back for a few years in childhood, rather than being pushed prematurely into professional-level situations. Parents and coaches should remember that youth sports, at heart, are for the enjoyment of the players.

Chapter 2

Is the "Student-Athlete" a Viable Idea?

THE UNIVERSITY OF CALIFORNIA, Los Angeles has always run strong sports programs. Under coach John Wooden, the men's basketball team dominated the National Collegiate Athletic Association's (NCAA) tournaments, winning ten championships in twelve years. UCLA's football, track, and swimming teams have also been successful. In all, UCLA has won more than ninety national titles in nineteen different sports. But the most unusual championship UCLA ever won was the women's national softball title in 1995. Not only was the title taken away two years later, but the way in which the Bruins won it was highly controversial.

With the season half over, an Australian named Tanya Harding (no relation to the American figure skater Tonya Harding) enrolled for the spring quarter at UCLA. Harding, then twenty-three, brought the Bruins to a new level of play. As a pitcher, she compiled a win-loss record of 17 and 1. Sparked by Harding, UCLA qualified for the national tournament. During the championship series, Harding allowed scarcely any runs and hit .500 besides, leading her team to the title. Harding collected her trophy as the tournament's most valuable player—and headed back to Australia two days later without taking her final exams. Her stay in California had lasted just ten weeks.

Controversy

Harding's whirlwind trip raised many eyebrows. "Ten weeks," wrote one commentator. "You wonder if she even brought more than one suitcase with her." The timing of Harding's midseason arrival and her departure before finals strongly suggested that Harding wasn't at UCLA to be a student. Rather, it seemed that she had been brought in to add experience and skill to a team that might not otherwise have contended for the national title. A "hired gun," some fans called her, though one reporter, noting the strength of Harding's arm, thought a better term would be "hired bazooka."

The Harding situation led to some troubling questions. College sports in America are supposed to benefit students who happen to be athletes. Indeed, the NCAA, which oversees college athletics, uses the term "student-athlete" to describe those who play college sports. In theory at least, athletic team members are in college for an education. They do sports as a sideline, much as a student who plays the trombone might join the school orchestra or a student who likes to act might try out for a play.

The guest appearance of Tanya Harding, however, seems to pervert that idea. She met the qualifications necessary to enroll at UCLA, but she was in no sense a student who happened to play sports. "Did she ever buy a notebook?" asked one writer. "Did she ever take a note? Did she ever take a test? If so . . . why?" Harding returned to the United States briefly that summer, as a member of the touring Australian national softball team. According to UCLA, she took and passed her finals then. She has not, however, given any indication of re-enrolling.

Rules and Ethics

UCLA officials defend Harding's participation on the team. A representative of the school points out that the young woman had every right to play softball for the university, even if she had no interest in academics. That is true. The NCAA has rule books that run to more than five hundred pages, and nowhere do the rules state that an athlete must pursue an education in addition to playing sports. A student who competes only for one quarter does not have to maintain a minimum grade point average, as most athletes do to remain eligible. And in the spring of 1997, when the NCAA stripped UCLA of its 1995 championship, the reason had nothing to do with the brevity of Tanya Harding's stay in Los Angeles. The university was found to have issued three more athletic scholarships to softball players than the rules allowed. UCLA refuses to say whether Harding was

Tanya Harding (right) is congratulated by her teammate at the end of a softball victory. Australian Harding played for the UCLA team for one quarter—a situation that many found unethical.

one of the players involved, but in any case the school's violation was not related to whether UCLA should have been allowed to use a nonstudent like Harding to begin with.

Still, many people believe that UCLA's recruitment of Harding violated the spirit of the rules. "While there are many top college athletes who depart without earning degrees," a journalist points out, "most stay longer than two months and muster at least a few academic credits along the way." Another writer, marveling at the short amount of time Harding had spent at the school, observes, "She surely didn't have time to learn the UCLA fight song. Or did she even know there was a fight song?"

UCLA supporters argue that no one was hurt by having Harding join the team. To a degree, this is true. Harding evidently came and went of her own free will. No critic suggests that the university some-how exploited her talent. For UCLA's competitors, though, the situation is a little different. Harding's presence on the UCLA roster may have deprived another school of the national championship. (The NCAA chose to list the title as "vacant" rather than award it to the runner-up.) While UCLA's actions may have been within the rules, most observers agree, they were scarcely ethical where opposing student-athletes were concerned.

And perhaps the unfairness extends even to members of Harding's own team. It may be a stretch to argue that every other UCLA softball player was primarily a student, but it seems safe to say that most felt more obligation to their studies than Harding. Might they have preferred a chance to prove their ability on their own? And even if Harding's participation on the UCLA team did not hurt her teammates and opponents, some argue, it still was hurtful—hurtful to the ideal of the image of college athletics and the ideal of the student athlete.

College Sports

College athletics covers a huge range. In some sports, notably football and men's basketball, the colleges with the top teams serve as the sport's minor league. Virtually all professional players play college ball before signing a contract. College is where they learn to play at a high level, where scouts see them in action, and where they play televised games in front of huge crowds.

Other sports, such as women's soccer and men's gymnastics, have much less appeal to the media and to fans. There is little chance for a player to turn pro and little opportunity for schools to peddle television rights and front-row seats. These athletes are much more likely to perform for small audiences, with no TV coverage.

With such a spread, it would be surprising if there weren't controversy in college athletics. The needs of a football player at one school are very different from the needs of a volleyball player or a fencer at another. To level the playing field a bit, the NCAA has divided colleges into categories based on their commitment to sports programs and the amount of money they are willing to budget on them. The schools that put the most money and emphasis on sports go in division I or IA; at the lowest level are the division III schools.

On top college football teams, a player's scholarship can easily translate into $100,000 or more over four years. Many colleges recruit players who have few academic skills.

These categories are used to determine league and championship groupings. There are also some differences in the way colleges at various levels can treat students. For instance, division IA schools give out a certain number of athletic scholarships per sport. These awards, such as the ones UCLA gave its softball players, are not based on a student's financial need, nor on his or her academic ability. Instead, they are given because of the student's athletic skills. Typically, they cover tuition, certain fees, and room and board. At an elite college such as Stanford University, the value of an athletic scholarship can easily exceed $100,000 over four years. Less intense programs provide fewer scholarships, and some smaller schools award none at all.

Student-Athletes

About three hundred thousand college students across the nation play interscholastic sports. Of these, many, if not most, are students who simply like to play: true student-athletes. The list includes the majority of athletes at division III schools, along with most who play the so-called minor sports. These students, indeed, are usually the first ones cited by supporters of college athletics. At Kenyon College, a small school in Ohio known for consistently strong swimming programs, student swimmers routinely go on to medical school, law school, and advanced study in nearly every liberal arts field.

But the situation is not so positive across the board. Many colleges have enrolled "students" who were not at all studious. Tanya Harding's case is an extreme example. A more common scenario involves scholarships awarded to athletes who are thoroughly unprepared for college-level academic work: teenagers who read on a second-grade level, whose high school grades are terrible, or who are far from emotionally ready to join a student body. There are plenty of athletes who fit this picture, compromising the ideal of college athletics.

The worst examples can be found in men's basketball and football, although, as Harding showed, they can exist in other sports, as well. In general, the larger the athletic program and the more popular the sport, the more likely it is that the ideal of student-athlete will be violated. The most blatant of these cases raise cries that athletes are being exploited, that schools' priorities are misplaced, and that college sports in general are in need of reform.

College athletes face off in an NCAA regionals game. In sports like basketball, few players are required to maintain a minimal academic standard.

Then and Now

Controversy about the role of student-athletes is nothing new. In fact, the notion of the student-athlete was corrupted more than a century ago. By 1890, many colleges were openly paying "tramp" players to join their teams. Some of these athletes even played for more than one school in a season. In 1902 the faculty at New York's Columbia University voted to make a football player ineligible due to poor grades. The athletic department did its best to overturn the decision, leading one college administrator to conclude that the football program was "incurable."

According to some, the situation is not much better today. Would-be reformers of college athletics focus on three specific areas in which the ideal is being corrupted. First, they disapprove of the way in which administrators and coaches recruit marginal students in their zeal to field winning teams. Second, they argue that the players are exploited for the university's gain and then tossed aside when their years of college eligibility are up. And third, they are concerned about the amount of money that pervades college athletics, money that seems to increase the pressures on schools to throw aside the goal of fielding teams of student-athletes: students who happen to play sports.

Any of these practices individually, critics of college sports say, is a perversion of the ideal. Taken all together, many observers find themselves agreeing with former University of Chicago president Robert Maynard Hutchins. Hutchins, in a very controversial move, dropped football from his school in 1939, stating that "a college which is interested in producing professional athletes is not an educational institution." For many reformers of today, as for Hutchins earlier in the century, the contradiction between big-time sports programs and the ideal of a university is too large to permit the existence on campuses of any sports activity beyond the purely recreational.

Unfit Students

"It is beyond question," says one writer, "that over the past half century many major college athletes have not belonged on a college campus." The University of Miami once fielded a football player who got 200 on the verbal section of the SAT college entrance exam. Two hundred is the lowest possible score, "the number you get for spelling your name correctly," as a journalist points out. Basketball player Chris Washburn scored the same and was nevertheless recruited by 150 colleges. Author Darcy Frey writes of college-bound basketball players who have never read a book from start to finish, or don't know how to solve simple multiplication problems.

Without their sports skills, these athletes would never have been accepted by a college. To some observers, this raises troubling ethical questions about the emphasis colleges put on sports. Even some colleges acknowledge that many of their athletes are unprepared for higher education. As an official at the University of Arizona admitted, "We recognize the farce of putting some of our [athletes] into regular classes with regular students." Yet if athletes are not "regular students," some ask, why are they there at all?

The NCAA has tried to regulate the admission of athletes to colleges. Besides meeting the admission standards of the school he or she attends, a student who wishes to participate in college sports must take several required courses in high school, achieve a minimum grade

Many college athletes cannot cut it in a classroom. Some have been unable to read at a high school level or perform simple math problems.

point average, and score at or above a certain level on a standardized college admissions test. The current standards, however, strike many observers as too low, so there have been several proposals to make admission standards for athletes somewhat tougher.

Many coaches and administrators, however, believe that accepting athletes who are not yet college material can do much more good than harm. They argue that a college education may be exactly what the athlete needs to get ahead. Several universities have strong remedial programs, designed to bring athletes along at their own pace and teach them what they failed to learn in high school and before. Even the least well prepared students are likely to learn something.

There is also concern that new admission standards would unfairly affect poor black athletes, who have tended to be the least qualified academically. As a result, when the NCAA has tried to make it harder for low achievers to receive athletic scholarships, it has been accused of classism and racism. Low scores on standardized tests do not necessarily imply laziness or lack of intelligence. As Darcy Frey points out, low test scores may instead be the result of poor teaching, cultural differences, or an underprivileged background. Frey and others believe that admission standards for athletes may actually be too high.

Success in College

Frey's arguments would be most convincing if student-athletes succeeded in college. In fact, many do. As of 1994, 58 percent of student-athletes could be expected to graduate from college eventually, in line with the graduation rate of 57 percent for all students. However, these figures may be misleading. Graduation rates vary depending on the size of the college and the sport. Athletes in minor sports at smaller colleges pull the graduation rates up. Big-time sports at large colleges are another matter. Only about 40 percent of male college basketball players ever get a degree. The rest drop out, fail, or finish their four years of eligibility without enough credits to graduate. At the University of Cincinnati, only seven basketball players out of several dozen graduated during a recent eight-year period. Not long ago, less than one out of ten University of Miami football players earned a diploma.

Source: NCAA, Division I Graduation Report.

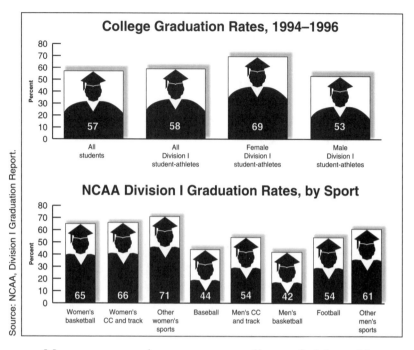

College Graduation Rates, 1994–1996

Percent	All students	All Division I student-athletes	Female Division I student-athletes	Male Division I student-athletes
	57	58	69	53

NCAA Division I Graduation Rates, by Sport

Percent	Women's basketball	Women's CC and track	Other women's sports	Baseball	Men's CC and track	Men's basketball	Football	Other men's sports
	65	66	71	44	54	42	54	61

Moreover, some observers accuse colleges of giving athletes a steady diet of easy courses leading to a worthless diploma. This prepares them for nothing, but makes the statistics seem better than they really are. Kevin Ross, a student at Creighton University, took courses like marksmanship and basketball theory. After four years at college, he still read on an elementary level. Such stories are not as rare as they should be. Too many athletes have "majored primarily in maintaining athletic eligibility," as one journalist puts it.

The shoddy educations given many athletes lead observers to conclude that the athletes are exploited for the university's gain. "I don't think the university really gives a damn about these kids," says one former NBA player about his college's basketball team. "I think they're just cannon fodder to win." This is especially a concern of students who are academically marginal to begin with. Many athletes finish their college eligibility and then discover that the college has made use of their talents without giving them any marketable skills in return. The environment of big-time college sports, concludes one journalist, chews up athletes who are unprepared for college life and spits them back out.

Recruitment

The student-athlete ideal is muddied in the area of recruitment of
athletes, as well. In their enthusiasm to put the best possible team on
the field, college coaches often cut corners or break rules to sign up
athletes they really want. Some coaches and their assistants offer
athletes almost anything to get them to attend their schools. According to NCAA rules, any gifts other than athletic scholarships are
expressly forbidden, but in fact much, much more is available. A
football player says he was paid $25,000 to come to Southern
Methodist University in 1983. The mother of basketball standout
Isiah Thomas remembers being offered hundreds of thousands of dollars by one coach, a beautiful house by another, airplane flights to her
son's games by a third—if she could get Isiah to play for them.
Coaches regularly ply high school stars with "cars, clothes, money
and women," as one observer puts it. At various times, up to one in
five NCAA schools is under investigation for recruiting violations.

*A college coach instructs his players on game tactics. Many coaches bend
the rules for star high school athletes, offering them cash incentives.*

And even legal recruiting tools often seem unethical. The basketball coach at the University of Southern California, for instance, admits to sending a thousand letters a *day* to prospects. A Fordham University assistant sent a high school senior a recruiting letter ending with the salutation "Health, Happine$$, and Hundred$." The competition for top-ranked players is fierce. In their desire to corral the best available players, coaches and athletic directors often forget that they are supposed to be looking for students who happen to excel at sports—not athletes who might or might not be college material.

Big Business

The ideal of the scholar-athlete is further corrupted because college sports, especially big-time football and basketball, are very big business. The financial stakes are great. CBS pays nearly $200 million for the right to broadcast the NCAA men's basketball tournament, and many schools take in thousands through ticket sales and other broadcasting fees. A trip to a major bowl game can be extremely lucrative for a football team. There is money to be made in college sports, and to many observers, college officials seem to lose all sense of proportion in chasing after it. In their desire to cash in on behalf of their institutions, some officials seem to substitute the goal of finding great athletes for that of finding great students. Then they put those athletes to work with the single-mindedness a professional coach would expect.

Money for college sports programs comes from other sources too. Some schools have local supporters and legions of alumni, or former students, who call themselves "boosters" of the college's teams. Most boosters are harmless, enthusiastic fans who follow the teams closely and donate modest sums of money to the athletic department. At a few schools, however, boosters have tremendous influence, spending freely (and often in violation of NCAA rules) to upgrade the sports program but losing sight of the goal of college sports.

Boosters typically provide the money and goods that go to athletes in recruitment schemes. Furthermore, boosters continue to give under-the-table cash payments to players even after they have arrived at school. In one survey, a third of athletes polled said they had received some pay-

ment while in college. Boosters were usually responsible.
The Southern Methodist University football program was
shut down for two years
because of repeated payments
made to players by fans.
According to the NCAA, the
school's administration knew
about the payments and did
nothing to stop them.

In some colleges, the
boosters often seem to be
running the athletic department. Worse yet, occasionally they appear to take over
the college administration.
Thus, boosters, not college
presidents, sometimes wind
up in charge of college
sports—and even colleges

*Sports teams are hugely popular with
alumni. Alumni sponsor booster clubs to
promote athletics exclusively. Thus,
many sports are fully funded while
academic programs are given short
shrift.*

in general. The NCAA reserves the heading "lack of institutional
control" to describe schools where booster factions have gotten out
of hand. Of the sixty-six colleges cited for rules violations during a
recent five-year period, forty-nine fit this category. College presidents of course ought to support the ideal of the scholar-athlete; they
are professional educators, after all. Booster clubs, however, exist
solely to promote athletics. Their bottom line is success in sports,
not in the classroom. In a sense, those forty-nine schools had thrown
the concept of student-athlete out the window.

Solutions

Restoring the innocence of college sports and the ideal of the student-
athlete is a daunting task. Many critics of athletic programs believe that
reality is so far from the goal that the gap can never be bridged. The most
obvious answer would be to de-emphasize big-time college programs.
But to many experts, this is like trying to put a genie back into a bottle.

"The athletes have become hired guns, mercenaries," says one college professor. "There's no such thing as amateur sports. Nobody believes it." "How do you de-emphasize?" asks another observer. "What do you do, tear down the [football] stadium and use it for the rodeo? They've found a way to make money at [college sports]."

But others are more optimistic. Some push for minor changes, others for more significant reforms. To address the woeful education some students receive, for instance, one legislator proposes linking graduation rates to a college's tax-deductible status. Schools that fail to graduate most of their scholarship athletes would suffer financially. Darcy Frey suggests stripping schools with low graduation rates of their division I classification, thus making them ineligible for major tournaments and TV contracts. Other proposals would put the burden of education on the colleges, not the high schools, by allowing universities to give scholarships to anyone they wanted—but students would have to demonstrate minimum academic achievement before they would be allowed to play.

Other reformers address the time commitment athletes must give to their sport. Training is so time-consuming and demanding, according to some experts, that it is unreasonable to expect a college athlete to take a full course load. Author James Michener, for instance, believes that athletes should take only one course during semesters when their sport is

A basketball player fends off an opponent to score. Critics believe that college sports must be reformed to link academic achievement to the ability to play.

in season. Another writer suggests that big-time athletes be given seven years to graduate. "When you go to college, you're not a student-athlete, but an athlete-student," agrees basketball player Isiah Thomas. Athletes, in this viewpoint, are shortchanged by the assumption that they are "normal" students.

Some critics go even further. They suggest that no amount of tinkering can rescue the student-athlete ideal. Journalist Douglas Looney, for instance, recommends that colleges simply pay their athletes. While "pay-for-play" would make college athletics indistinguishable from professional sports, Looney argues that too often there is no real difference anyway. Moreover, the athletes are often the only people who do not share in the money that big-time sports can bring. From a fairness standpoint, the pay-for-play idea makes sense to many observers.

At the opposite end of the spectrum, perhaps the furthest extreme, a handful of commentators argue for disbanding big-time college athletics altogether, pointing out that no other nation gives the responsibility of training athletes to colleges. In the ideal world of these critics, professional football and basketball would run their own minor leagues, colleges would abolish athletic scholarships, bowl games and TV contracts would be outlawed, and sports would be played informally at colleges between groups of student-athletes—just the way they were intended.

College administrators have any number of choices. They can make sports that attract big-time recruiters more professional, or they can try to reduce the emphasis on them. They can give more help to athletes who are marginal students, or they can redefine the rules to keep marginal students out. Or, of course, they can make no changes at all. Whichever way college administrators choose to go, they will be guided, at least in part, by their feelings about the idea of the student-athlete. The debate about college sports comes down to whether the concept of the student-athlete is a workable one. The way in which administrators decide this issue will determine whether reform will occur at all, and if it does, how such changes will be handled.

Chapter 3

How Does Drug Use Corrupt Sports?

DURING THE 1996 SUMMER OLYMPICS in Atlanta, Irish swimmer Michelle Smith was the talk of the pool. Smith entered four individual events, winning three and finishing third in the other—perhaps the single most impressive performance of the Games. Not only was Smith's accomplishment remarkable, it was statistically unlikely as well. No Irish woman had ever won an Olympic medal of any kind. Moreover, Smith was twenty-six, quite old as competitive swimmers go, and she had not had much success before. One observer described her swimming career as "dog-paddling in mediocrity." Smith was taken so lightly before the Games began that a sports magazine, predicting winners for Smith's races, never even mentioned her.

Smith's feats delighted the Irish, along with many other people around the world. "She has surpassed everything that has ever been done in Irish sport," said a government official once the Olympics were over. "The whole country's going mad," said an Irish reporter after Smith won her first gold medal. "No work is being done. . . . The whole country's stopped." One of Smith's American fans cited her as a role model for hard work and perseverance, while another described her approvingly as a "dedicated athlete from a small, poor country."

But not everybody was delighted. Many observers, especially some American swimmers and coaches, voiced suspicions about the reason for Smith's sudden, last-minute improvement. By the time she had won the second of her gold medals, rumors were flying

Michelle Smith of Ireland competes in the 1996 Summer Olympics. Many suspected that Smith's success was related to performance-enhancing drugs, even though she never tested positive for such substances.

around Atlanta that Smith's achievements were not simply due to talent and drive. Instead, competitors charged, Smith was using a drug to help her swim faster.

Cheating?

The charges, if true, were serious. Many chemicals can build muscles, increase stamina, and accelerate growth—precisely what an athlete needs to be stronger and faster. Some of these chemicals, such as the male hormone testosterone, or human growth hormone, occur naturally in the body. Taking more of them than the body produces on its own will lead to an increase in strength or speed. Many artificial chemicals, such as anabolic steroids, have the same effect. In the world of sports, these chemicals are called "performance-enhancing drugs."

The use of performance-enhancing drugs, however, is forbidden. At the Olympic Games, all medal winners are routinely tested for signs of these substances (or abnormally high levels of those which occur naturally). Many other competitions require drug testing as well, and top athletes must also undergo random tests. Any world-class competitor can expect plenty of urine tests aimed at determining whether his or her body has more of a performance enhancer than it should. A positive test can mean suspension or outright banishment from competition—not to mention giving up any medals that might have been won.

To some observers, signs of drug use by Michelle Smith were clear. Smith had made so much improvement in so little time that no other explanation seemed to make sense. Her biological clock was evidence too; at an age when nearly every other champion woman swimmer was retired or in decline, Smith was setting personal bests. "We've never seen anybody go from [age] 24 to 26 the way she has," said John Leonard of the American Swimming Coaches Association. "Every bit of circumstantial evidence [of drugs] is there."

Others agreed. "Any time any person from any country has dramatic improvement," said U.S. swimmer Janet Evans, "there is that question." Richard Quick, the coach of the American women's swim team, was even more blunt. "We've given people the benefit of the doubt for too long," he said as Smith won one medal after another. "It's time we investigate sudden jumps in performance."

Smith's Response

Smith has steadfastly maintained her innocence. "I have never used performance-enhancing drugs," she said flatly during the Olympics. She attributed her improvement to several factors: a new and better diet, harder work, recovery from health problems, and most of all a new training regimen. She also scoffed at the idea that her performance in Atlanta was a surprise, pointing out that she had been ranked second in the world in two of the events just the year before. "It hasn't been an explosion," she said. "It's something I've been working on the last three and a half years."

Indeed, drug tests on Smith in Atlanta revealed nothing. And Smith reminded observers that she had been tested frequently with never a positive result. "I'm probably the most tested Irish athlete," she said at the Games. "For every one time a person on the U.S.

Michelle Smith wears her third gold medal of the 1996 Summer Olympics for winning the 200-meter individual medley. Were accusations of Smith's drug use just sour grapes by the losers?

team has been tested, I've been tested five times." While the numbers may not have been exact, her point was well taken: the American swimmers, in fact, had not been tested nearly as often as Smith.

Smith attributed the accusations to sour grapes. Evans failed to win a medal in Atlanta, and while the U.S. women's team as a whole did unexpectedly well, Smith noted that she had beaten out some favored Americans. "When somebody else is successful," she said during a press conference, "and your own swimmers aren't quite as successful, it's very easy to point an accusing finger." Others agreed. Smith's "crime," wrote one American, was "winning three gold medals that were apparently American property."

By the time the Atlanta Olympics were over, Michelle Smith was known throughout the sports world. Officially, the question of whether she used drugs to win her medals is closed. According to state-of-the-art tests, she did not. Nevertheless, rumors and doubts persist. The situation disturbs many people. If Smith was cheating, then other swimmers were unfairly deprived of medals and glory. If she was not, then her accomplishments have been unfairly tainted.

And sport itself has lost something during the debate as well. Smith's case demonstrates how far the sports world has come from the ideal of pure sportsmanship. Both the use of drugs and the accusation of drug use corrupt the notion of sport as a competition of skills. "Any great performance in swimming now has a cloud over it," says U.S. coach Quick. "That's sad." Sad for Smith, sad for swimming fans, and sad for every athlete who suddenly does much better than expected.

Performance Enhancers

The use of performance-enhancing substances is not new. As early as 1869, cyclists attempted to increase their endurance by mixing heroin and cocaine, which were not then illegal. Other chemicals with a history of use by athletes include the potentially poisonous drug strychnine, caffeine in huge doses, and opium. As science grew, so did knowledge of newer and more effective drugs. At present there is a bewildering array of substances said to increase an athlete's ability to perform. Nearly all are banned. The U.S. Olympic Committee (USOC), for instance, issues a nine-page booklet listing *some* of the substances forbidden in international competition. The list ranges from asthma medications and the pain reliever Novocain to some herbal teas. American athletes are strongly encouraged to check with the USOC before taking *any* medication.

While many substances can improve an athlete's performance, a few stand out. Chief among them is the class of drugs known as anabolic steroids. Artificial substances that increase muscle growth, steroids were originally developed to help patients with protein and bone deficiencies. However, around 1950 scientists discovered that steroids had a positive effect on athletes as well. While studies don't precisely agree, there seems to be no question that—as one reporter put it—steroids "pump you up fast, increase your speed, decrease the time it takes to rebound from a serious workout, and often make you as ferocious as Mike Tyson with a bloodied nose."

According to many insiders, steroid use is widespread among both men and women athletes. Steroids first were used by bodybuilders and weight lifters. "By the 1960s," says one observer, "it was virtually a given that nearly all world-class weight lifters used steroids." The drugs soon became common in other sports that demand strength and endurance, notably football, swimming, cycling, and track and field. Steroids were officially banned in international competition in 1970. But two years later an American track and field competitor polled his Olympic teammates to find how

many had used steroids. About two-thirds had used them within the previous six months.

And the problem has only gotten worse. Among football players, estimates of steroid use range from three-quarters of all linebackers up to half of all players. "Everyone in cycling dopes himself," a professional cyclist said a few years ago, "and those who claim they don't are liars." Michael Mooney, a California bodybuilder who has advised many top-flight athletes on steroid use, goes even further. "I would say nearly every top-level athlete is on something," he says.

Dangers of Drugs

However, steroids are far from safe. They have physical side effects most people would choose to avoid. Women who use steroids are prone to develop a deep voice and facial hair. "I've been off the drugs for almost two years now," remarks a female powerlifter who gave up steroids, "but I still have to shave every day." Men's testicles may shrink, and their breasts may grow. Any steroid taker risks liver damage and kidney failure, as well as high blood pressure, diabetes, tendon injuries, and a host of other medical problems. Several retired athletes blame constant poor health on steroid abuse. Lyle Alzado, a football player who died in 1992 from a brain tumor, had attributed his cancer to the steroids he took daily for nearly twenty years.

Steroids cause mental and emotional distress too. "It definitely makes a person mean and aggressive," says a football player with personal experience of steroid abuse. His wife agrees. "He's so impatient when he's on the steroids," she says. "He becomes vocal and hostile real fast, and he never was that way before." Episodes of sudden drug-related violence are so common, they even have a name: "'roid rages." "Five of the guys on our team went on [steroids] at the same time," reports the football player. "A year later four of them were divorced and one was separated."

The effects of other performance enhancers are as bad or worse. Amphetamines can impair a user's judgment and increase his or her hostility too; moreover, they can be addictive. A hormone called erythropoietin, or EPO, occurs naturally in the body but has been produced artificially as well. It increases the number of red cells in the bloodstream, thus allowing the body to carry and use more oxygen. In addition, however, EPO can make the blood thick enough to clog the heart, forcing it to stop. Over the last few years, artificial EPO has been implicated in the deaths of *two dozen* young athletes, mostly Dutch and Belgian. Other substances abused by athletes can cause diabetes, strokes, and comas.

THE CONSEQUENCES OF STEROID USE

Below is a listing of the various health problems and conditions caused by steroid use. These consequences have been grouped according to gender.

In males
- impotence
- breast enlargement
- sterility
- shrinking of the testicles
- enlargement of the prostate gland, which can lead to difficulty urinating

In females
- irreversible male-pattern baldness
- irreversible lowering of the voice
- menstrual irregularities
- decreased breast size
- irreversible and excessive hair growth on body

Source: National Federation of State High School Associations.

And dangerous performance-enhancing chemicals can come from an athlete's own body. So-called blood doping, recently banned by the International Olympic Committee, is a process in which athletes inject themselves with about two pints of stored blood shortly before an event, again increasing the number of oxygen-bearing red blood cells. Undesirable effects of blood doping include allergic reactions, hepatitis, and kidney damage.

The Decision to Dope

Drugs and procedures like blood doping are forbidden in competition. Their use raises troubling ethical concerns. And they have negative effects on health. So why would athletes consider them? Because "people are looking for any kind of edge," says a specialist in sports medicine. The desire to win at any cost is at the root of the craze for drugs.

Many athletes and observers attest to this. A physician who has served the U.S. weight-lifting team speaks of athletes' obsessive desire to excel: "If I'd told people back then that rat manure would make them strong, they'd have eaten rat manure." Others agree. "The overwhelming majority of athletes I know," says an Olympic champion, "would do anything, and take anything, short of killing themselves, to improve athletic performance." Several studies go even further. In 1967 over a hundred top American athletes were asked whether they would take a substance knowing that it would make them an Olympic champion but might kill them within a year. More than half the sample said they would. Similar studies have been repeated since then, with similar results.

And once a few top athletes begin using drugs, the pressure on others to do the same becomes intense. Not taking a drug that other competitors are using makes it doubly hard to win. "I knew it was illegal," says a German athlete who started with steroids at the age of seventeen, "but everybody was taking them." As a San Diego football player told his team physician, "I'm not about to go one-on-one against a guy who's grunting and drooling and coming at me with big dilated pupils [classic symptoms of steroid use] unless I'm in the same condition."

Pressure also may come from coaches and trainers and even from parents. In former East Germany, steroid use was routine.

"You didn't ask questions," said one swimmer. "It was just the normal way of life." Of the U.S. high school athletes using steroids, about one in five say that a coach or teacher recommended the drug. And a few American parents, concerned that their sons or daughters lack the necessary strength to succeed in sports, have actually provided steroids for their children. In such cases, it can be hard for athletes to say no.

Drug Testing

Over the years, various tests have been developed to ferret out competitors who use steroids and other illegal drugs. Virtually all these tests involve the analysis of a urine sample provided by the athlete. Testing has been refined to the point of revealing minuscule amounts of a substance. Some equipment is so sensitive that it can detect a cube of sugar dissolved in a swimming pool.

Drug tests are awkward, expensive, and embarrassing to athletes, but they can work. Several world champions have had to forfeit titles during the last thirty years, most notably 1988 Olympic sprinter Ben Johnson. And the prospect of drug testing has caused other athletes to change their minds about participating in certain competitions. In 1983, for instance, tests caught a number of cheaters during the first few days of the Pan-American Games. Twelve American athletes who had not yet competed left for home as soon as they heard the news. "None admitted to steroid use," writes an observer, "but

A chemist tests urine for the presence of performance-enhancing drugs. Such testing is imperfect, as some athletes switch to less detectable substances.

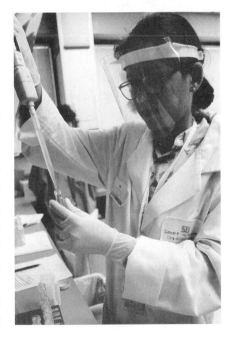

it was difficult to imagine that athletes of their calibre suffered simply from homesickness."

Unfortunately, urine tests are far from perfect. Several banned substances, such as EPO and human growth hormone, cannot yet be detected by any urine test. A few water-based steroids are hard to detect. Only twenty-four hours after ingestion, no trace of them can be detected in the urine. Even random testing is of little help here. Blood tests would be more accurate and perhaps less humiliating for the athletes, but the cost at this point is prohibitive.

It is also possible to cheat in a urine test, and many athletes know how to do it. College football players swap stories of the cleansing effects of certain kinds of tea. "It wipes everything clean in your system," one player contends, if it's drunk about four hours prior to a test. Other methods include passing off someone else's urine as your own (this backfired on one male athlete whose urine test revealed that the person who had provided "his" sample was pregnant) and taking substances that hide the presence of drugs. There are higher-tech ways as well. "Drug testing is a joke," says a coach who deals in steroids as a sideline. "The people who are smart and have the money to pay for drugs can easily pass." A doctor agrees. "No athlete I've ever helped has tested positive," he says, "and I've helped hundreds."

Drug testing would probably be more accurate if more money were spent on developing procedures. However, most nations and competitions do not give the subject high priority. Germany, Canada, and Japan are three countries that do take testing seriously; indeed, an extremely sensitive test developed by the Japanese found traces of steroids in many Chinese swimmers not long before the 1996 Olympics. The U.S. sports community, on the other hand, has been accused of poor enforcement of rules. While the USOC refuses to give out exact figures, there seems to be little question that less money is spent on drug testing in the United States each year than in Canada—a much less populous country.

The USOC conducts a few random spot checks, but puts most of its energy into testing athletes just before they leave for the Olympics. Some people argue that this policy leaves the impression that the USOC is more interested in avoiding forfeited medals than in making sure athletes are drug-free. In part, some experts feel, this is because the USOC prefers not to risk alienating sponsors and fans who want to believe that Olympians—or at least American Olympians—are clean.

Other Testing Concerns

There are further problems with drug testing as well. A few people raise privacy issues. Random testing, especially, offends some observers, who suggest comparisons to a police state. Rights may get trampled when athletes are accused of drug use. Some doctors and athletes say testing is the wrong way to go for another reason. At present, great amounts of time and money go into fighting drug use, but perhaps the resources would be better spent in teaching about nutrition and the body, to demonstrate that drugs are not the athlete's only way to improve sports skills.

In any case, a positive test does not always mean that an athlete tried to cheat. Sometimes an athlete is a victim. Ludmila Engquist, a Russian hurdler now competing for Sweden, was banned from competition for four years after failing a drug test. During this period, it was learned that Engquist's former husband had spiked her protein supplement with steroids in hope that she would be caught and punished. When the truth came out, the ban was revoked, but Engquist had already suffered damage to her reputation and lost valuable competition time.

And tests may be just plain inaccurate or misleading. More recently, American track stars Sandra Farmer-Patrick and Mary Slaney were found to have suspiciously high levels of testosterone in their bodies. The athletes argue that they happen to be individuals who produce these abnormal levels naturally. In fact, a handful of women do, but the condition is so rare that some believe the two athletes should be banned anyway (as of this writing, Farmer-Patrick has been given a four-year suspension); others argue for giving the women the benefit of the doubt.

Moreover, the list of banned substances is so long that even officials can't be sure what is legal and what is not. In the 1996 Olympic Games, several athletes were disqualified for using a stimulant called bromantan. On further review, however, it was determined that bromantan was not formally banned at all. Yet a positive drug

Runner Sandra Farmer-Patrick (left) was suspended for four years after a suspiciously high level of testosterone was found in her body—thought to be the result of illegal doping.

test can ruin a career, and may be ruining careers of some innocent people as well as those who intended to cheat.

But the biggest concern right now is that drug testing misses many, perhaps most, of the athletes who break the rules. Indeed, some question whether testing will ever accomplish all its supporters desire. At a cost of up to $150 for a single urine test, the price alone is prohibitive. Even if tests were foolproof, "we cannot test everybody, everywhere, every time," says a Canadian medical officer. And as long as testing remains flawed, some athletes will get away with cheating.

"Downright Cheating"

"Cheating," most agree, is exactly the right word. "That's what taking steroids is all about," says a British weight-lifting official: "cheating, downright cheating." Another observer puts it even more strongly. "When athletes who have taken steroids compete against athletes who have not," he says, "it's taking money from them. It's theft." An athlete who uses drugs has an unfair advantage over his or her opponent. As a result, the use of performance enhancers raises deep ethical questions for sports.

The ideal is that sports events are contests between the bodies, skills, and wits of two competitors or teams. Where drugs are concerned, the ideal is polluted. "Doping," writes Miguel Angel Bermudez Escobar, a sports administrator from Colombia, "runs counter to the very nature of sport." With drugs, the contest becomes one of pharmacist versus pharmacist as much as athlete versus athlete. "Last year," an American weight lifter said in 1971, "the only difference between me and [world champion Vasily Alexiev] was that I couldn't afford his pharmacy bill. Now I can. We'll see which are better—his steroids or mine." Drug use, as one scientist remarks, "degrades sports into a biochemical challenge."

It may never be possible to develop an all-purpose drug test. It may not be possible to keep athletes from looking everywhere for an edge—even when they seek advantages from illegal and harmful substances. "You can't stop it," says a publisher of a sports magazine. "It would be absolutely naive to think you could."

Should sports officials therefore stop banning drugs, or trying to wipe them out? A few observers argue that this would be the best course

Weight lifting is another sport plagued by performance-enhancing drugs such as steroids. Such drugs create an unequal playing field between players who use the drugs and those who abide by the rules.

of action. It may be better for sports, they say, to have drug use accepted and out in the open, banishing instead the hypocrisy of pretending it isn't happening because athletes are careful to conceal a forbidden practice. Moreover, they say, banning a substance makes it appealing. "That tells the athlete that this drug improves performance," says a testing official, "or we wouldn't ban it." And a handful see no ethical problems with steroids and other drugs at all, likening them to other training aids at an athlete's disposal. Steroids, writes one commentator, are no worse than Gatorade or Nautilus equipment. "Many of the means and ends which athletes use and seek are unnatural," he points out.

But for most sports fans, allowing drugs would be an unacceptable surrender. Unlike Nautilus equipment, which offers an environment for hard work, not a substitute for it, drug use provides a boost that hours of training can never match. Drug use creates health problems. It unfairly penalizes athletes who choose to stay clean. It puts undue pressure on competitors to bulk up by any means possible. As in the case of Michelle Smith, it leads to accusations of cheating leveled at anyone who unexpectedly performs especially well. Drug use, in short, perverts sports and the ideal of fair and true competition.

The goal of sports is not to set ever better world records by any means possible, nor to create an artificial athlete in the drugstore or lab. Doping "sullies the image of sport and casts a shadow over sporting events," writes Bermudez Escobar, the Colombian administrator. Even if the ideal is corrupted, it is still better to have an ideal than to have none at all. For Bermudez, and for many other people involved in the sports world, giving in to performance-enhancing substances could never be an option.

Chapter 4

Do Men and Women Have Equal Access to Sports?

IN THE SPRING OF 1991, Brown University made a decision that would shake the sports world. The long-established Ivy League school, located in Providence, Rhode Island, was losing money, and university president Vartan Gregorian had asked virtually every department on campus to cut back on spending. In particular, he had asked the athletic department to trim about $115,000 from its budget for the coming academic year. Athletic director David Roach cut some general expenses and four entire teams, feeling that he had no other options. On April 29, Brown announced it would drop men's water polo, men's golf, women's gymnastics, and women's volleyball as varsity sports, starting with the 1991–92 school year.

Spending cuts are usually controversial, and the cuts affecting the sports teams were especially so. Some students organized a boycott of the annual athletic awards banquet. "There was no consideration given to the athletes," complained a volleyball player. Most coaches and players had no idea that cutting their programs was even under consideration: the announcement "came as a complete shock to me," said the head volleyball coach.

Faced with these complaints, Brown tried to smooth things over. The school pointed out that the defunded teams could still compete and use school facilities. The only change was that the university would stop providing money for uniforms, travel, and coaches' salaries. To some, however, Brown's actions seemed like a betrayal. "I was completely devastated," said a gymnast.

But complaints and devastation soon gave way to anger, especially among the women whose sports had been cut off from funds.

A volleyball player wondered why athletic director Roach had sin-gled out four sports for the brunt of the cuts and left others more or less alone. "An athletic director should be someone who cares about every sport," she said. "Roach doesn't." As time went on, anger intensified. In April 1992 several volleyball players and gymnasts filed suit against Brown, charging that the university had discrimi-nated against them because they were women.

Discrimination Suit

The students based their argument on Title IX of the federal Educa-tional Amendments of 1972. Title IX, which bans discrimination "on the basis of sex" in any educational program that receives fed-eral funds, covers nearly all elementary and secondary schools, pub-lic and private, and colleges as well. From its beginning, the law has been applied to sports programs. Any school that gives unequal treatment to men's and women's sports is subject to be challenged under the provisions of Title IX, and the students argued that Brown's decision was in violation of this law.

Although the Brown student body in 1991 was roughly half female, well over half of the varsity spots available to Brown athletes were on men's teams. If drastic measures were needed, some of the students said,

Title IX required Brown to target only men's teams, at least until the number of women athletes equaled the number of men. At a school where half the students were women, they argued, Title IX mandated that half the sports program be devoted to women.

Whether women's sports teams should receive similar advantages in funding and other opportunities remains controversial.

Brown fought back. School administrators repeated their statement that the teams could continue without college funding. It was inaccurate, they argued, to talk as if the teams had been dropped completely. Moreover, the men's golf and water polo teams had more participants than the women's volleyball and gymnastics squads. Thus, more men than women were feeling the brunt of Brown's cutbacks. Finally, Brown argued that Title IX required only a commitment to take women's sports seriously—which, administrators said, Brown did. "Brown's program of athletics for women is indisputably one of the nation's largest and best," said one university official. Brown was so certain of winning that when lawyers for the athletes offered to settle the case out of court, Brown refused. And when a judge ordered Brown to reinstate funding for the two women's teams until the case could be heard, Brown fought that decision too.

Three Issues

The case wound very slowly through the legal system. By law, the judges were required to consider three questions. First, did Brown provide fair opportunity for the women on campus to participate in sports? Second, had Brown worked to expand its options for women in recent years? And third, was Brown making an effort to "accommodate the interests" of women athletes? According to standard Title IX guidelines, a school would be held to be in violation of the law only if it failed all three tests.

According to the students' lawyers, the answer was clear: Brown failed. As evidence, they cited the difference between the percentage of female students at Brown and the percentage of female spaces set aside for varsity sports. Though Brown's student body was 51 percent female, only 38 percent of athletes were women—a difference of thirteen percentage points, not close to the five-point difference the federal government typically accepts as a practical measure of equality.

The students also pointed out that women on campus were interested in several sports that Brown had never offered on a varsity level, sports such as fencing and skiing. Therefore, they argued, Brown was not trying hard enough to "accommodate the interests" of women. Nor, after defunding two teams, was the university making progress toward meeting women's needs. Attorney Lynette Labinger said that the situation was simple. "If the courts rule for Brown," she said, "women lose."

The university disagreed. While continuing their earlier arguments, lawyers for Brown also brought up new ones in court. First, they said that Title IX didn't require precisely equal representation on men's and women's teams. Instead, the real question was whether men and women were represented according to their interest in sports. Brown presented research claiming that about 60 percent of its students who wanted to play sports were men—a figure, administrators pointed out, that almost precisely matched the percentage of varsity slots Brown reserved for male athletes.

According to Brown, interest was the only fair way to determine equality. "A program that is truly non-discriminatory," athletic director Roach wrote, "would attract six men for every four women." Mandating equal numbers would lead to unfairness. "I could easily have 50 men trying to play baseball, while the women's softball team will have positions vacant," he continued. Indeed, Brown argued, a strict 50 percent goal amounted to a quota system. If more men than women wanted to participate in sports, that was not the university's fault.

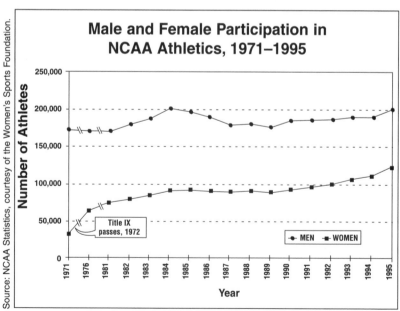

Source: NCAA Statistics, courtesy of the Women's Sports Foundation.

Brown also insisted that there simply was no more money left to fund teams. "Brown cannot and will not devote any additional . . . funds to athletics," university president Gregorian said during the trial. Any further money given women's sports, then, would come directly from funds allotted for men's programs. The university reluctantly said it could trim a few spots from team rosters, but Roach said that Brown would not "water down" its men's teams, implying that a few sports would have to be dropped completely instead. Roach and others pointed out that cutting men's sports to achieve equality was hardly what Title IX was designed to do.

"Plain, Old-Fashioned Sex Discrimination"

But the students and their lawyers rejected Brown's arguments. Responding to Brown's assertion that more men than women like sports, the lawyers claimed that women tend to compete less frequently than men because they have not yet had the chances men have had. As for the prospect of Brown's being forced to cut men's sports, the lawyers felt this was an empty threat. "To say 'We have no other options,'" Lynette Labinger argued, "is silly for people with that level of sophistication." In fact, Labinger and her team of lawyers insisted that Brown should have to come up with a plan that did not involve cutting men's budgets.

In 1995 U.S. District Court Judge Raymond J. Pettine ruled in favor of the students, writing that the true test of Title IX compliance is whether sports participation "substantially mirrors" the student body. Lawyers for the students cheered this ruling. Pettine's decision, one lawyer said, showed that Title IX is not about mandating quotas but about eliminating "plain, old-fashioned sex discrimination."

Brown appealed—and lost again. "We view Brown's argument that women are less interested than men . . . with great suspicion," the appellate judges wrote. "This is not an affirmative action case." Instead, the judges said, the case was about fairness, and Brown had indeed acted unfairly in cutting the funding for the two women's teams. Brown appealed once more, this time to the U.S. Supreme Court, but in April 1997 the high court refused to hear the case. Thus, the decision in favor of the students was allowed to stand.

Attorney Lynette Labinger represented female athletes in a suit against Brown University for treating women athletes unfairly.

Women's Sports Before Title IX

If open access to sports is part of the ideal of competition, then the recent past demonstrates failure at reaching that ideal. Before Title IX's passage in 1972, access to sports for women was usually bad and occasionally nonexistent. In 1971, according to a well-known study, one high school girl out of twenty-seven participated in interscholastic sports. Lack of interest may have played a part, but more significant were cultural attitudes against girls who competed. A few years before Title IX, for instance, a Connecticut judge ruled against a girl who wanted to run cross-country. "Athletic competition builds character in our boys," the judge wrote. "We do not need that kind of character in our girls." Money was an issue too. In Syracuse, New York, for instance, the school board spent $90,000 on boys' teams during 1969, and $2,000 on girls' programs. The following year there was a budget deficit. The boys' programs were cut back by $3,000. The girls' programs were eliminated.

The situation was not much better at the college level. Just after Title IX was passed, the University of Washington spent about $2.5 million on men's sports, $18,000 on women's. At Vassar College in Poughkeepsie, New York, the men's budget was twice the women's in 1972. This was particularly startling because Vassar, traditionally all female, had had no male students at all just five years earlier. A mid-1970s booklet about equality in sports mentions a university that spent nothing whatsoever on women's sports. These imbalances were not unusual—and before Title IX, they were perfectly legal.

The few women who did participate in sports encountered many obstacles. Except for a handful of cases, notably basketball in Iowa, women's sports were basically ignored. At Austin Peay State University, women athletes had no budget for lodging or food on the road. The students who played in away games bought their own meals and curled up in opponents' gyms overnight. An athlete from another college remembers riding to games in beat-up old vans while the men's teams rode a luxury bus. At another school, women students could not use the handball court unless a man signed up for them. A high school women's basketball team practiced only on days when the boys did not need the gym. At many colleges and high schools, this was standard procedure.

Pushing Towards Equality

Title IX has made a huge difference in sports. There is no question that women are much better off than they were a quarter-century ago. At Georgia Tech, where women make up only 27 percent of the student body, 31 percent of varsity athletes are women—a proportion that was unheard-of in 1972. In a recent five-year period, American colleges nationwide added eight hundred new women's teams, while the figure for men's teams actually dropped. In 1994 alone, fifty-nine colleges added women's soccer teams. The women's collegiate basketball tournament is now televised nationally. And women's crew— but not men's—is a championship sport at the college level.

Still, supporters of Title IX complain, the basic imbalance persists. Although there are more women athletes than ever, more than 60 percent of spots on varsity college teams are still reserved for men. The NCAA predicts that equity of participation probably will not be achieved before about 2008—thirty years after Title IX's

A woman athlete in a relay race pushes herself to the maximum for her team. Title IX requires that colleges fund men's and women's sports equally.

original 1978 deadline. Georgia Tech is the only large school in the United States at which the percentage of women athletes is higher than the percentage of women students. Most of the schools with more or less equal numbers have been forced to achieve equity by losing a Title IX discrimination case. "You pick a school and I'll bet it's in violation" of Title IX, says one expert. As for the televised basketball championships, observers argue that coverage does not necessarily imply equity. Women have to play at odd times to get their games broadcast; men do not.

And participation rates usually are better than several other measures of fairness. "The test for genuine equity," writes a journalist, would be a demonstration "that men would be happy to swap resources with women. But they would be fools to trade." Only about a quarter of the money spent on college athletics goes to women's sports. Coaches of women's teams routinely get lower salaries than their colleagues who coach men's teams. At schools such as the University of California, Santa Barbara, women still typically take twelve-hour bus trips while the men's teams fly. In

Knoxville, Tennessee, a high school girls' soccer team had to fight to be allowed use of the school football field—but an under-ten boys' football team had no trouble getting permission. In Owasso, Oklahoma, the school board built a state-of-the-art baseball stadium for boys' use, and converted an old Little League park for the girls' softball team. The unfairness rankles many observers. "How can I expect my daughter to believe she can be whatever she wants to be," asks a parent whose daughter's school refused to fund softball, "when I let her go to school and hear, 'No, you can't'?"

"It's Not Always Fair"

A substantial number of people argue that Title IX has gone too far. Some are cautious in their criticism of the law. "Title IX is an admirable goal," says a men's track coach whose program has fewer resources than the women's program at his college. "However, in practice it's not always fair." Others are more outspoken. "Men need sports more than women," claims a water polo coach whose program was cut back in 1991. He calls Title IX "buffoonery."

The issue Brown raised about women's interest levels continues to come up. "Young men are losing the opportunity to compete," complains an Illinois congressman; he proposes giving questionnaires to students, as Brown did, to serve as a basis for determining the percentage of money that will be given to each gender. But many supporters of Title IX reject this line of thinking entirely. Donna Lopiano of the Women's Sports Foundation cites figures suggesting that girls and boys are equally interested in sports up to age nine; she blames the dropoff after that mainly on the gap in school spending.

Other coaches have complained that Title IX unfairly hurts men's sports. Indeed, many schools have cut back on men's sports, especially those that do not bring in money. Over the last decade about a dozen colleges have dropped men's swimming, for instance, and more than fifty wrestling programs have disappeared. Men's gymnastics, tennis, and lacrosse teams have also been victims of cuts. Athletic directors echo David Roach's argument that Title IX gives them no choice.

Football programs are also an issue. College football teams are huge, often exceeding a hundred athletes, and they are all-male. No

Men's college football is one of the most popular of all sports. Some feel that Title IX does not take into account a sport's popularity or the relative lack of female interest in sports.

comparable women's sport attracts such numbers. This is a sore point for some football coaches. Title IX "penalizes institutions that sponsor football," says a representative of the College Football Association, "because there's no matching sport for women in terms of participation." A school that has a football team must find a way to provide an extra hundred or so slots for women. But rather than spend so much money on sports which bring in little or no revenue, a few schools have chosen instead to drop football altogether.

Men, Women, and Football Players

According to some supporters of Title IX, football coaches' opposition to the law stems as much from a desire to keep their budgets intact as it does from sexism. Not only does football use many athletes, it is also by far the most expensive sport at the college level. In fact, football eats up more money than all women's sports combined. A recent study found that the largest colleges spent an average of $29,000 per player on their football teams, almost three times the average of other programs' per-player costs. Given such numbers, many Title IX defenders are suspicious of colleges that claim to be unable to divert any more money to women's sports. "One fair way to achieve equity quickly," suggests a journalist, "would be to trim those bloated 85- to 100-man squads, reduce their scholarships, [and] fire all those superfluous coaches."

In response, a number of coaches have pressed for laws that would make football exempt from Title IX legislation. In this model, there would be three programs: men's sports, women's sports, and football. The first two would have to be equal, but the third could be larger. Thus far, however, this argument has gone nowhere. Indeed, when the University of Texas was sued for Title IX violations, the school used this notion to defend itself—and lost. And after the Brown decision, it seems unlikely that the coaches' position will carry the day.

Supporters of Title IX generally disapprove of cutting men's sports to reach equality. They would rather see women's sports opportunities improved. The point of the law, says Donna Lopiano, is to bring women up to the level of men, not to bring men down to the level of women. But most advocates for equity agree that in the course of attempts to achieve a balance, men's sports may be cut. During recent congressional hearings on Title IX enforcement, says Christine Grant, the athletic director at the University of Iowa, "there was a fair amount of sympathy for the men who were losing their teams." Grant understands this view, but wonders, "Where is all the sympathy for the women who have never, ever *had* these opportunities?"

Pro Sports

Title IX's influence has already gone far beyond schools. Even without laws to enforce participation, more and more women and girls are competing in sports of all kinds. In the 1976 Olympics, six of every seven American athletes were male. In 1996 the figure was down to four out of seven. There is now an all-woman professional baseball team, and two women's pro basketball leagues have recently begun play.

Even here, however, there is debate over the amount of access women truly have to sports. Youth league sports are often beset by Title IX–type problems. A basketball coach in Florida, for instance, asserts that girls in her league get less expensive T-shirts, fewer games, and worse playing conditions than the boys. For adults, the situation is not necessarily better. Until very recently, Lopiano points out, newspaper sports sections did a more thorough job of

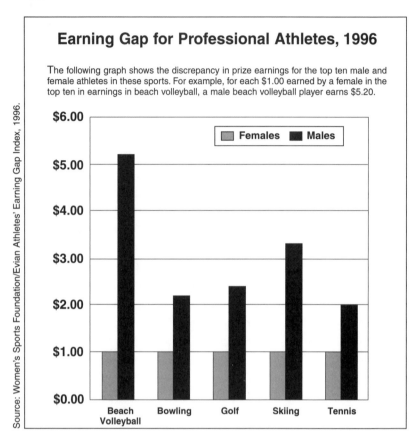

Earning Gap for Professional Athletes, 1996

The following graph shows the discrepancy in prize earnings for the top ten male and female athletes in these sports. For example, for each $1.00 earned by a female in the top ten in earnings in beach volleyball, a male beach volleyball player earns $5.20.

Source: Women's Sports Foundation/Evian Athletes' Earning Gap Index, 1996.

covering horse and dog racing than women's athletics. Media coverage of the women's professional basketball leagues has been spotty thus far. The *New York Times* ran a feature on the American Basketball League (ABL) during its 1997 championship series—but did not publish any box scores.

Moreover, some observers say that women's sports will never be truly popular. To date, women have not watched women's sports in great numbers. A national magazine says women "appear to lack the manic sports-spectator gene." That leaves men, and indeed the audience for televised women's basketball is more than half male. But some men refuse to watch women's sports because they view women athletes as less skilled than male athletes and therefore less exciting to watch. And even men who appreciate women's sports may be reluctant to attend games in person. The wife of one male fan found that many of her friends distrusted her husband's motivation for watching female athletes. They suspected that he went to the games because he was interested in "ogling young women running around a field in short skirts," as she put it.

Nevertheless, advocates for equity are cheered by the inauguration of the new leagues. Many fans find they appreciate women's sports because of the emphasis on teamwork, rhythm, and crisp play. "At the Olympics," says television host Bob Costas, "women's basketball was much more interesting to watch." Plenty of fans agree. "It's more competitive," says a male fan about the ABL; "I can live without the slam dunks," says a woman. Other fans point to superior effort, enthusiasm, and attitude among the women. Money plays a role too. Tickets to women's sports are cheaper than corresponding tickets to men's games, and it is easier for fans to believe that the lower-paid women "play for the joy of competition," as one journalist wrote.

Women have never watched sports in the same large numbers that men do. In fact, the audience for women's sports is more than half male.

Corporate Funding

And money plays another role as well. Corporations have discovered women's sports. From McDonald's to Nissan, businesses are racing to sponsor the new professional leagues. "Corporate sponsors aren't only returning our calls," says a founder of the ABL. "They're calling us *first*." Three new magazines for sports-minded women were introduced in 1997 alone. There is a booming market in sports equipment for women, too. Adidas has come out with a women's soccer shoe. Spalding has developed softball mitts and basketballs suited to women's hands. "Sporting-goods manufacturers," says a journalist, "simply can't *afford* to ignore female athletes any longer."

But perhaps the most significant sign of growing equity lies in the attitudes of the youngest generation. "Boys are growing up with an appreciation of what girls can do," says a broadcast executive. "There's an appreciation for who girls are." Donna Lopiano agrees. "People under 40—men and women—are all in favor of girls' getting the chance to play sports," she says. "The fathers had grown up in sports, and so they wanted their daughters to have the same opportunities." To be sure, many young men seem to respect women athletes more than their fathers and grandfathers did. "I'm not about to step into the batter's box against *her*," says a Princeton baseball player about his girlfriend, a pitcher on the university's softball team.

As the Brown decision shows, the struggle for equity continues. In a few colleges, however, the fruits of victory in these battles are clearly visible. Kansas University is home to one of the most successful men's college basketball teams of all time. It also has one of the highest percentages of varsity women athletes of any division IA school. The University of Florida combines championship football teams with recognition from *Sports Illustrated* as the best college in the country for women's sports. Many observers are optimistic. "There'll be no turning back," writes one expert. "The male domination of sports is a washout." "We have arrived," says basketball star Nancy Lieberman-Cline.

Gender equity, at heart, is about an ideal of sport—the ideal of fairness. "If I pay $10 [in taxes to the school athletic program]," says an Oklahoma father, "$5 ought to go to my boy, and $5 ought to go to my girl. To me, it's simple math." Ideally, sports are about teaching values, concentration, and teamwork—goals just as valuable for girls as for boys. "If sports are a way to educate the young," says former U.S. representative Cardiss Collins of Illinois, a sports fan all her life, "they have to be for males *and* females." There is little debate that these words are true—that sports should be open and available to all. The question that continues to divide society, even after the Brown decision, is how best to achieve these goals.

Chapter 5

Do Athletes Make Good Role Models?

F EW ATHLETES ARE AS FAMOUS or as controversial as basketball player Dennis Rodman. On the up side, Rodman has overcome great adversity to get where he is. Recognized as one of the finest athletes in his sport, Rodman has regularly been among National Basketball Association leaders in rebounding, and his tenacious style of play has helped lead his teams to several league championships.

But Rodman has been characterized as a loose cannon. He has been in trouble with team and league officials for offenses such as missing practices, removing his shoes on the bench, and refusing to join his teammates in a huddle. More seriously, he has head-butted a referee and kicked a camera operator during a game. During the 1996–97 season he was suspended twice, once for the kicking incident and once for swearing during a live television interview. Nor has Rodman's personal life been any calmer. He has become well known for dyeing his hair unusual colors and for dressing in women's clothing. Rodman has had a marriage that lasted less than three months, has fathered an out-of-wedlock child, and says he has attempted suicide.

Still, Rodman is among the most popular athletes in the nation. His autobiography, *Bad as I Wanna Be,* was a best-seller. He is a commercial spokesman for many companies who are willing to overlook the player's antics in exchange for being associated with him. Sports stores across the country do a huge business in Rodman souvenirs. "We're sold out of his jerseys," says one clerk. "We get a dozen every two weeks, and we can't keep them in the store."

A Good Role Model?

But Rodman's popularity concerns many experts. Rodman, they say, is a terrible role model. His behavior, on and off the court, sets a poor example for children. "If kids want to protest to their parents about not buying the latest [athletic shoes]," syndicated columnist Mike Lopresti writes sarcastically, "they can always kick something

Dennis Rodman is ejected from a game for his second technical foul. The antics of stars such as Rodman make many question his suitability as a role model.

until it turns blue." Many commentators worry that Rodman's style
sends the wrong message: that immoral or dangerous behavior is
acceptable. "This is definitely not a man that I want my son to have
as a role model," says a father.

Even those who admire Rodman's style of play worry about the
effects his antics have on children. "There are an awful lot of young
people out there," President Bill Clinton said after the incident with
the cameraman, "who don't have an immediate positive male role
model who can contradict a lapse by an athlete." While describing
himself as "a big Dennis Rodman fan," Clinton appealed to Rodman
to set a better example and apologize for his misbehavior.

But being a role model, Rodman argues, isn't his job. "I thought
all along I was a basketball player," he writes in his autobiography.
"You don't pay me to be a guardian angel. . . . You pay me to play
this game." According to Rodman, the public should not ask him to
be something he is not. "We're athletes," he argues. "We're not
equipped to run somebody else's life. That's not our occupation."
Some fans agree with him. "So he has a temper," one fan says.
"Who doesn't? I think that we should just let the man do what he
does best: play ball."

Still, many commentators are not convinced. By virtue of being
a star basketball player, they say, Rodman influences children,
whether he wants to or not. In a sports-crazy world, athletes *are*
heroes. They *are* larger than life. What they do on and off the court
affects the children and teenagers who admire their athletic skills.
Along with a multimillion-dollar contract and countless endorsement opportunities, critics argue, comes a responsibility to fans,
especially to children who watch the games. Rodman has been very
clear in stating the position that athletes should not have to be role
models; but not everyone agrees.

The Ideal

In fact, athletes have always been considered role models. Over the
years, many athletes have been respected not just for their skills, but
for their dedication to their work, their sense of sportsmanship, and
their exemplary lives on and off the playing field. Sports figures
such as early twentieth-century baseball pitchers Walter Johnson

Early twentieth-century professional athletes, such as baseball pitcher Walter Johnson, cared about providing a positive role model for children.

and Christy Mathewson have often been cited as heroes in their own time: excellent models for any child, interested in sports or not.

Johnson, for instance, "was not only a legendary pitcher," writes baseball historian Bill James, "but the incarnation of the athletic virtues of decency, charm, and style." He was applauded for his gentle nature, his generosity to teammates, and his horror of ever hitting a batter with a stray pitch. Mathewson is remembered in much the same way. A memorial plaque called him "the greatest pitcher of his era" and went on to add that "he won the admiration of his opponents and the affection of a nation." It was said of Mathewson that umpires sometimes asked his opinion on a close play involving his own team—and trusted his honesty in making the right call.

Ideally, all athletes would be like Johnson and Mathewson. But even in the early years of sports, many—perhaps most—were not. Baseball star Ty Cobb, who played often against Johnson, was a mean man and a dirty player hated by teammates and opponents alike. First baseman Hal Chase, who played briefly on a team managed by Mathewson, conspired with gamblers to lose games on purpose. It is hard to imagine a worse corruption of the ideal of sports. Other athletes were selfish, greedy, rude to fans—and the list goes on.

"It's an Honor"

There are certainly many sports figures today who take their jobs as role models seriously. They make it a rule to behave as responsible members of society. "Athletes aren't as gentlemanly as they used to be," says golf star Tiger Woods. "I like the idea of being a role model. It's an honor." Many athletes visit children in hospitals, attend summer camps, distribute game tickets to underprivileged kids, or work in soup kitchens. "Kids are really into sports and sports figures," says volleyball player Bob Ctvrtlik. "I know the kind of impact a visit from an athlete can have."

Unfortunately, not all athletes can measure up to these standards. Some sports figures project an attitude of selfishness or lack of respect for opponents and society. Rather than using their fame to help their communities, they seem to be mostly interested in promoting themselves. The effect of these players' behavior on children worries many observers. In some youth leagues, for instance, players refuse to shake hands with opponents after games or spit in their hands before shaking—disrespectful actions many experts feel were

A player autographs baseballs for young people. Children often idolize star athletes, and many parents worry that they will emulate unsportsmanlike behavior that many such athletes exhibit.

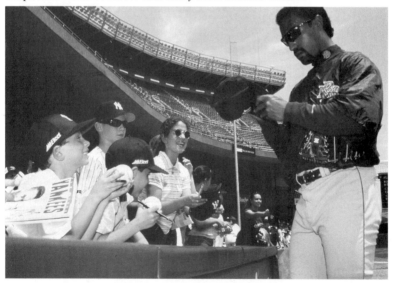

learned from watching famous sports figures like Rodman. "Trash-talking" to opponents has become much more frequent in high school games over the last decade or so, and it is increasingly common to find young athletes, from tennis players to figure skaters, who throw tantrums about every negative ruling by a judge or referee—just like their favorite professional.

Worse, many poorly behaved athletes are stars whose playing style is copied by children on basketball courts, ice rinks, and athletic fields across the country. The athleticism and grace of these players may be worthy of admiration, but the whole package often seems lacking. At the heart of the debate about role models are individuals whose talent is not matched by their maturity.

"Belle Does What He's Paid to Do"

Some observers believe that in today's world, it is unfair to ask athletes to be anything more than highly skilled at sports. Sociologist Harry Edwards says that athletes are simply "entertainment celebrities" who have no obligation to serve as anyone's hero. Columnist Deron Snyder cites Albert Belle of the Chicago White Sox as an athlete whose behavior on and off the baseball field makes him a poor role model. However, as Snyder points out, Belle does what his employers hire him to do—drive in runs. "He's not paid to make people feel good about him, his sport or his peers," Snyder says.

To people like Edwards and Snyder, a player's skills are all that matter. As long as a player continues to do what he does best, he is worthy of respect; no attention should be paid to problem behaviors. For some fans, this forgiving attitude extends to brushes with the law. "He's a good running back," says a young fan about former University of Nebraska football player Lawrence Phillips, whose legal troubles include charges of assault and drunk driving. "It didn't bother me what he did." When another football player, Dallas Cowboy Michael Irvin, arrived at the courthouse after being arrested on drug charges in 1996, court personnel joined hundreds of fans in trying to get the athlete's autograph. They may have disapproved of Irvin's drug use, but he was still one of the best football players in the country.

And many players question why fans look for their heroes among those unlikely, for whatever reason, to prove worthy of their respect. "How did you function before I got here?" Rodman asks pointedly of those who think he should be a more positive model. Many athletes are uncomfortable with the idea that their athletic skills—or even their good works—make them somehow deserving of status as a hero. "I'm just a person," says Colorado Rockies baseball star Larry Walker. "What's the big deal?" Michael Irvin's teammate Emmitt Smith is a widely respected athlete who flatly rejects the idea that he should serve as a role model. Instead, he encourages children to look closer to home for people to emulate. "What's wrong with listening to your mama," he asks, "or your daddy, or your brother and sister, or your teacher, or policemen and firemen and doctors and lawyers?"

Celebrity Status

But for many observers, it's a cop-out to say that athletes are not obliged to be role models. Unlike teachers, police officers, firefighters, and doctors, athletes are constantly in the public eye. No one pays to watch mothers and fathers do their jobs; sports figures, on the other hand, perform in sold-out stadiums, appear constantly on television, and—perhaps most important—rarely complain about their fame and fortune. "Athletes are perfectly willing to be endorsers, spokesmen, icons and symbols," points out columnist Mike Lopresti, citing sports celebrities who make millions of dollars from advertisers in addition to their regular salaries. It is unfair, he argues, for athletes to insist that they are "only athletes," while at the same time shoe companies, television stations, and replica jersey sales build them into something bigger.

Lopresti's is a common point of view. "Athletes can't have it both ways," a newspaper editorial agrees. "They can't accept the million-dollar salaries and the national spotlight, without the responsibility of squeaky cleanliness that goes along with superstardom." Sports figures are famous not simply because they are outstanding athletes; they are also famous for being famous. They are public figures whose every move is scrutinized. "The players may not want to be idolized, but they are," another journalist says. In this view, athletes who behave outrageously have a responsibility to tone down their acts—a responsibility to themselves, to society, and most of all to their fans.

Acting Like Idiots

Other writers, however, have argued that fans actually encourage bad behavior. If fans find athletes lacking as role models, they say, the fans themselves are to blame for placing the players on too high a pedestal. Too many athletes appear to have learned the wrong lesson: from their experience, they have concluded that their skills make them better human beings than everyone else, so ordinary rules do not apply to them. According to most journalists who covered the Michael Irvin drug case, Irvin did not understand the seriousness of

A fan raises his arms in an enthusiastic salute for his team. Many decry the unsportsmanlike behavior that today's young athletes are allowed to exhibit in professional sports.

"OKAY....I'LL SWAP YOU TWO DRUG USERS AND A GAMBLER FOR ONE
DRUNK DRIVER AND AN ACCUSED DOUBLE-MURDERER...."

his actions. One writer, watching the public fawn over Irvin at the courthouse, realized why. "The justice system couldn't teach Irvin a lesson," he wrote. "He was still fabulously popular because he was a Cowboy."

Irvin is not alone. Men such as former tennis player John McEnroe, says columnist Joan Ryan, "seem to feel that success entitles them to act like idiots." In some ways, it did. Fans continued to support McEnroe through his many temper outbursts on the court and the disparaging comments about referees and other players he made off it. Former pitcher Tom House writes about baseball stars such as New York Mets Keith Hernandez and Dwight Gooden, whose drug problems were readily forgiven by hometown fans. "A more ordinary player" charged with similar offenses, he observes acidly, "endures a nightmare's worth of boos and jeers."

"Pitchmen with 'Edge'"

According to some observers, though, the problem goes beyond hometown fans—it permeates American culture. "Society rewards the antihero," says a television commentator, "and it's a shame." Although golfer Fuzzy Zoeller recently lost a lucrative endorsement contract for making a racist joke, companies rarely drop controversial athletes who have been hired to push their products. Rodman, for instance, has no shortage of endorsement offers. "Corporate

America would rather have pitchmen with 'edge' than squeaky clean role models," a journalist complains. "Who says boorish behavior will cost you marketing opportunities?" Baltimore Orioles baseball star Roberto Alomar, who spat on an umpire late in the 1996 season, did not lose a single endorsement deal. Many observers are made uncomfortable by the rewards given to star athletes who seem to be anything but good role models.

Baltimore Orioles baseball star Roberto Alomar spits on an umpire. Alomar continues to make millions with endorsement deals from corporations who do not see his behavior as a reason to pull him from endorsing their products.

Compounding the problem is the unwillingness of some sports administrators to take a clear stand against poor behavior on and off the field. Roberto Alomar's punishment—a five-game suspension, to be served at the beginning of the 1997 season—struck many observers as far too mild. "How do you tell your kids to live by the rules," asked news correspondents Cokie and Steve Roberts after the incident, "when a rich and famous athlete gets away—literally—with spitting in the face of authority?"

Alomar is not the only example. Many athletes escape serious consequences for offenses on and off the field. "We pamper our athletes," a writer noted, "pay them millions and forgive them their sins, all of which sends a message." When sports heroes get away with a slap on the wrist instead of a serious penalty for misbehavior, "we're telling kids there's a separate set of rules for different people," complains a psychologist. "It destroys a real sense of right and wrong."

Moreover, teams, like fans, often seem willing to ignore all sorts of behavior to take on a player who might carry them to a league championship. "Can you hit home runs?" asks House. "Fine, we'll overlook that drunk-driving charge." And, perhaps, give you a higher salary. "Be like Albert," a commentator wrote sarcastically when the White Sox signed Belle to a huge contract. "Anger and arrogance pay well."

Safety and Privacy

Athletes today live extraordinarily public lives, and there is a certain cost attached. To some observers, this cost helps explain why athletes are not good role models. It can be wearying, or worse, to be in the public eye all the time. Dennis Rodman wants to be recognized wherever he goes, but many other athletes do not. Former St. Louis Cardinal pitcher Bob Gibson, for instance, has written that it is the height of rudeness to interrupt a player at a restaurant to ask for his autograph—yet many fans think nothing of it. The crush of publicity is so strong that baseball player Cal Ripken travels under an assumed name when his team is on the road, and Michael Jordan cannot go for a walk in the park without being mobbed. Star athletes are unable to lead normal lives, and may come to resent it.

Nor is the only worry one of privacy. Tennis player Monica Seles was stabbed at a tournament several years ago. She missed many months of competition and has not yet fully regained her previous form. Tiger Woods is one of a number of athletes said to travel with personal bodyguards. But as players distance themselves from fans, it becomes harder for fans to identify with them.

And the amount of money athletes make also separates them from the rest of society. The average salary for a baseball player is well into six figures. Superstars such as Jordan, golfer Arnold Palmer, and boxer Evander Holyfield make more in a year than most people will earn in a lifetime. When athletes buy sports cars, mansions, and private jets the way the average fan buys bags of potato chips, there is a gap, and the potential for anger. Some fans jealously calculate a player's earnings per hit, touchdown, or goal scored. One baseball writer, mentioning a team that seemed to fail frequently in the clutch, called the players' problems sad, but not tragic. "They are too well paid for tragedy," he explained.

Not only does anger over money strain the relationship between athlete and fan, it also makes it hard for a fan to relate to a player as a hero. A true hero, many fans feel, would not switch teams as a free agent simply for a better financial deal elsewhere, as many players do. In fact, one of the most loved and respected athletes of recent times is retired baseball player Kirby Puckett of the Minnesota Twins, who accepted less money in order to remain loyal to the team he'd always played for. Still, considering the public scrutiny athletes receive, perhaps the money represents a fair trade.

The Future

What can be done to bring back the Walter Johnsons and Christy Mathewsons of sport? Ideally Americans might de-emphasize sports, diminishing in turn the corrupting influence of money and fame. But it seems hardly realistic or fair to ask athletes to give up most of their salaries simply so fans can identify with them more easily. And athletes *are* famous. As Harry Edwards says, athletes are entertainers. They are young, talented, and appealing to kids. It seems unlikely that sports will fall out of favor anytime soon.

Still, there are small steps athletes and fans might take to help make sports figures become better role models. First, perhaps, would be to follow the lead of organizations such as the Citizenship

Through Sports Alliance. This group, formed in early 1997, includes members of the U.S. Olympic Committee and all four major sports leagues, along with high school and college sports administrators. Its mission is to promote the positive values that underlie sports: respect, teamwork, and leadership.

Sportsmanship is a major goal of the group's programs. So is the recognition that players may need help becoming effective heroes for children. "Teaching sportsmanship," editorialized a magazine that applauds the formation of the alliance, "is as important—*more* important—as teaching the jump shot or the double-play pivot." If teaching sports is about instilling values, as many commentators suggest, then it makes sense to teach those values explicitly, as a central part of sports instruction.

Another, more cynical, suggestion is to ignore bad behavior by athletes. "It would be nice, for once, to see him ignored," Mike Lopresti writes about Rodman. "Left to sit on the sideline in silence, with the plug pulled on the Dennis Show." Instead of bemoaning an athlete's flaws, this argument runs, let him be who he is without getting excited about it. "Rodman and his skits are only important if we let them be," Lopresti says. We would not be up in arms about Albert Belle, writes a

Texas Rangers pitcher Nolan Ryan signs autographs for fans. Ryan has always provided a sterling role model for children and adults alike.

young fan, "if the media and the fans only focused on his playing." To a degree, in fact, many fans already do this. Plenty of children and teenagers wear Rodman jerseys, admire his style of play, and even appreciate his willingness to be his own man—without dyeing their hair to match his or otherwise trying to emulate the player's lifestyle.

And finally, society can focus on the men and women of sport who *do* lead exemplary lives, on and even off the field. Television and newspapers can cover the exploits of athletes who show hard work and persistence, who use their fame and fortune to help make the world a better place, who speak with humility about their skills and with respect about their opponents. Among these heroes, active and retired, who have been singled out in letters, Internet postings, and news articles during the last year are baseball players Nolan Ryan, Bernie Williams, Pam Davis, and Dave Valle; tennis players Boris Becker and Chris Evert; track star Jackie Joyner-Kersee; hockey players Mario Lemieux and Wade Redden; basketball players Katrina McClain, David Robinson, and Terrell Brandon; football players Steve Young and Danny Wuerffel; softball player Dot Richardson; and many, many more.

Fans Celebrate a True Role Model

But chief among them, perhaps, is Baltimore Orioles infielder Cal Ripken. In September 1996, Ripken broke a baseball record that many fans thought would never be broken. That night, Ripken played in his 2,131st consecutive game, surpassing the 2,130 played by New York Yankees legend Lou Gehrig. The Orioles game was delayed for many minutes in the fifth inning while fans and players alike celebrated. Ripken acknowledged the crowd and took a lap around the field.

"There on the field, during the game," a columnist wrote afterward, "opponents were shaking Ripken's hand, and it was right." Ripken was being celebrated for his talent and durability, of course, but many people felt that the celebration was at bottom about far more than that. Playing in over two thousand consecutive games is a feat of the will as much as of skill. It is an achievement of courage and determination along with fielding and hitting. Ripken had refused all opportunities during his streak to take a day or two off, to rest a nagging injury, or to sit down against an especially tough pitcher. Instead, he had played day in and day

Baltimore Oriole Cal Ripken waves to the crowd after tying Lou Gehrig's record of 2,130 consecutive games.

out, giving the fans their money's worth. He was, most fans agreed, a true role model.

That night in Baltimore, Ripken was celebrated for his loyalty, his bravery, his focus and drive, and—perhaps most of all—for his willingness to set an example for all society. "For one brief moment," the columnist wrote, "no one was reluctant or embarrassed to acknowledge what we valued." Moments like these serve as reminders that sport is about far more than greed, cheating, and gold medals. Long after the scandals of 1996 are forgotten, the achievement of Cal Ripken will be remembered.

Perhaps all fans have to do is learn to focus attention on the good rather than the bad. Perhaps athletes do not have a responsibility to be heroes. Perhaps, instead, fans have a responsibility to find and support the athletes who, like Cal Ripken, truly represent the best of humankind.

ORGANIZATIONS TO CONTACT

The following organizations are involved with the issues described in this book. Each offers publications and makes other information available to the public. (All names, addresses, and phone numbers are subject to change.)

Center for the Study of Sport in Society
Northeastern University
360 Huntington Ave., 161 CP
Boston, MA 02115
(617) 373-4025

The center is mainly interested in the relationship between sports and society at large. It develops programs that identify problems and promote solutions in sports-related areas.

Knight Foundation Commission on Intercollegiate Athletics
John S. and James L. Knight Foundation
One Biscayne Tower, Suite 3800
2 S. Biscayne Blvd.
Miami, FL 33131
(305) 908-2600

The Knight Commission was established to study problems in intercollegiate athletics and to propose solutions.

National Association for Girls and Women in Sport
1900 Association Dr.
Reston, VA 20191
(703) 476-3400

This organization focuses primarily on meeting the needs of

coaches, administrators, and athletes involved in girls' and women's sports programs.

National Association of Intercollegiate Athletics (NAIA)
6120 S. Yale Ave., Suite 1450
Tulsa, OK 74136
(918) 494-8828

The NAIA promotes and develops intercollegiate athletics as an integral part of colleges' educational mission.

National Collegiate Athletic Association (NCAA)
6201 College Blvd.
Overland Park, KS 66211
(913) 339-1906

The NCAA oversees most intercollegiate athletic programs in the United States.

National Federation of State High School Associations
11724 NW Plaza Circle
PO Box 20626
Kansas City, MO 64195
(816) 464-5400

This organization oversees many high school athletic programs in the United States.

National Youth Sports Coaches Association (NYSCA)
2050 Vista Pkwy.
West Palm Beach, FL 33411
(800) 729-2057
NYSCA's focus is on youth sports. The organization attempts to ensure that organized athletics are a positive experience for all children who take part.

Women's Sports Foundation (WSF)
Eisenhower Park
East Meadow, NY 11554
(800) 227-3988

WSF promotes the participation of women in sports and works to educate the general public about athletic opportunities for women.

FOR FURTHER READING

Michael Bamberger and Don Yaeger, "Over the Edge," *Sports Illustrated,* April 14, 1997.

Ira Berkow, "A. B. L. Has Nonstop, Hard-Nosed Action," *New York Times,* March 8, 1997.

H. G. Bissinger, *Friday Night Lights.* Reading, MA: Addison-Wesley, 1990.

Geoffrey Cowley and Martha Brant, "Doped to Perfection," *Newsweek,* July 22, 1996.

Tom Donohoe and Neil Johnson, *Foul Play: Drug Abuse in Sports.* Rev. ed. Oxford: Basil Blackwell, 1989.

Allan Guttman, *A Whole New Ball Game.* Chapel Hill: University of North Carolina Press, 1988.

David Hill, "A Pitch for Equality," *Teacher,* August 1996.

Leslie Brown Kessler, "When a Fan Is Just a Fan," *Newsweek,* October 7, 1996.

Douglas S. Looney, "Cash, Check, or Charge?" *Sporting News,* July 1, 1996.

Steve Lopez, "Thrown for a Loss," *Sports Illustrated,* January 20, 1997.

Donna Lopiano, "Issues in Women's Sports: The 1997 Story," Women's Sports Foundation, http://www.lifetimetv.com/WoSport/TOPICS/PAR_TR/97issues.htm, 1997.

Buster Olney, "Shortstop's Bright Future Fades to Black," *New York Times,* May 30, 1997.

Karen N. Peart, "Not Just a Game," *Scholastic Update,* April 12, 1996.

Aric Press, "Old Too Soon, Wise Too Late?" *Newsweek,* August 10, 1992.

Marty Ralbovsky, *Destiny's Darlings.* New York: Hawthorn, 1974.

Skip Rozin, "Steroids: A Spreading Peril," *Business Week,* June 19, 1995.

Joan Ryan, *Little Girls in Pretty Boxes.* New York: Doubleday, 1995.

Kathleen Sharp,"Foul Play," *Ms.,* September/October 1993.

Sports Illustrated, Letters, February 17, 1997.

Oliver Trager, ed., *Sports in America: Paradise Lost?* New York: Facts On File, 1990.

Alexander Wolff, "Breaking Through," *Sports Illustrated,* December 2, 1996.

WORKS CONSULTED

Dave Anderson, "Suspicion Surrounds a Swimmer," *New York Times,* July 23, 1996.

Miguel Angel Bermudez Escobar, "Doping—A Shadow over Sport," *Unesco Courier,* December 1992.

Madeleine Blais, *In These Girls, Hope Is a Muscle.* New York: Atlantic Monthly Press, 1995.

Joe Bower, "Sweat Equity," *Women's Sports and Fitness,* January/February 1997.

Martha Brant, "Pool Sharks," *Newsweek,* August 5, 1996.

Brown (University) Daily Herald, many issues, 1991–present.

Julie Cart, "NCAA Hits Bruins Hard," *Los Angeles Times,* May 7, 1997.

Larry Dorman, "To Be Young, Gifted, and Tormented," *New York Times,* April 8, 1997.

Jerry Fraley, "Lone Star," *Inside Sports,* November 1996.

Ron French, "Is Ex-Piston Rodman a Spectacle or 'an Out-of-Control Role Model'?" *Detroit News,* May 13, 1996.

Darcy Frey, *The Last Shot: City Streets, Basketball Dreams.* Boston: Houghton Mifflin, 1994.

Ed Hinton, "Crash but No Smash," *Sports Illustrated,* April 14, 1997.

Tom House, *The Jock's Itch.* Chicago: Contemporary Books, 1989.

Barbara Kantrowitz, "Don't Just Do It for Daddy," *Newsweek,* December 9, 1996.

Leslie Kaufman and T. Trent Gegax, "Prime-Time Players," *Newsweek,* February 10, 1997.

Dave Kindred, "We Need a Little Respect," *Sporting News,* February 10, 1997.

Robert Lipsyte, "Fighting On in the Battle for Equity," *New York Times,* April 27, 1997.

Norman Lockman, "Gymnasts' Gold Medal Not Worth Risk," *Poughkeepsie (New York) Journal,* August 1, 1996.

Jere Longman, "The Wearing of the Gold Is All That Matters to Smith," *New York Times,* July 26, 1996.

Mike Lopresti, "It's Time to Stop Giving Rodman Any Attention," *Poughkeepsie (New York) Journal,* January 31, 1997.

Steve Marantz, "A Man's Appreciation of Women Athletes," *Sporting News,* February 24, 1997.

Ken McMillan, "Local Colleges Making Strides in Support of Women Athletes," *Poughkeepsie (New York) Journal,* March 9, 1997.

James Michener, *Sports in America.* New York: Fawcett Crest, 1976.

Leigh Montville, "Ringer from Down Under," *Sports Illustrated,* June 12, 1995.

National Collegiate Athletic Association, *NCAA Committee on Infractions Summary of Cases.* Booklet: Overland Park, KS: NCAA, 1997.

Andrew Phillips, "A Haunted Past," *Maclean's,* July 27, 1992.

Janet Podell, ed., *Sports in America.* New York: H. W. Wilson, 1986.

Ron Rapoport,"Thompson's Attack on Prop 48 Is Wrong," in Dave Sloan, ed., *Best Sports Stories, 1990.* St. Louis: Sporting News, 1990.

Peter D. Relic, "Back to the Field of Dreams," *Independent School,* Fall 1996.

Bill Reynolds, *Fall River Dreams.* New York: St. Martin's Press, 1994.

David Roach. "Will Title IX Be the End of Equal Opportunity in Sports?" *Washington Post,* October 5, 1995.

Randy Roberts and James S. Olson, *Winning Is the Only Thing.* Baltimore: Johns Hopkins University Press, 1989.

Dennis Rodman, with Tim Keown, *Bad as I Wanna Be.* New York: Delacorte Press, 1996.

Steve Rushin, "Inside the Moat," *Sports Illustrated,* March 3, 1997.

Joannie M. Schrof, "A Sporting Chance?" *U.S. News & World Report,* April 11, 1994.

Deron Snyder, "Forget the Critics, Belle Is Baseball's Free-Agent Treasure," *Baseball Weekly,* November 6–12, 1996.

Mark Starr, "No Credit for UCLA," *Newsweek,* June 12, 1995.

_____,"On the Beam," *Newsweek,* June 10, 1996.

Chris Stewart, "Toxic Coaches Poison Our Youth Sports," *Poughkeepsie (New York) Journal,* October 14, 1996.

Laurie Tarkan, "Unequal Opportunity," *Women's Sports and Fitness,* September 1995.

Ian R. Tofler et al., "Physical and Emotional Problems of Elite Female Gymnasts," *New England Journal of Medicine,* July 25, 1996.

U.S. Olympic Committee, *USOC Guide to Prohibited Substances and Methods.* Booklet. Colorado Springs: USOC, 1997.

Steve Wilstein, "Big Money in College Sports Could Result in Lots of Change," *Wilkes-Barre (Pennsylvania) Times Leader,* December 26, 1996.

Tom Witosky, "Equity Cuts into Men's Programs," *Poughkeepsie (New York) Journal,* March 9, 1997.

Alexander Wolff, "Broken Beyond Repair," *Sports Illustrated,* June 12, 1995.

Chris Wood, "The Perils of Doping," *Maclean's,* July 27, 1992.

Don Yaeger and Douglas S. Looney, *Under the Tarnished Dome.* New York: Simon and Schuster, 1993.

INDEX

Picture Credits

ABOUT THE AUTHOR

Stephen Currie is the author of close to thirty books, including *Adoption* (Lucent Books' Overview series), *Music in the Civil War, Birthday-a-Day, Problem Play*, and *We Have Marched Together.* Under the name Tristan Howard, he has written five volumes in the Leftovers series about an incompetent kids' sports team. His interest in sports dates to the age of seven, when he attended a baseball game between the Chicago Cubs and the St. Louis Cardinals; he played baseball throughout his childhood and was a competitive swimmer in high school. He lives in Poughkeepsie, New York, with his wife, Amity, and children, Irene and Nicholas, both of whom play youth soccer.